AF797755

The Sovereign Wallet: Blockchain, AI, and Personal Financial Freedom

Master next-generation returns : Your essential guide to secure self-custody, AI-optimized DeFi and tokenized asset yields.

Disclaimer
The author has received no compensation, sponsorship, or other consideration from any company, protocol, project, or individual mentioned in this book. No official relationship —financial, advisory, or otherwise—exists between the author and any entity referenced herein.

All information, data, strategies, and examples are presented to the best of the author's knowledge and belief as of the date of publication. Blockchain technology, decentralized finance, and cryptocurrency markets evolve rapidly; prices, protocols, security practices, and regulatory environments may change without notice. Readers are solely responsible for verifying the current accuracy and applicability of any information before acting on it.

This book is for **educational and informational purposes only**. It is **not financial, investment, legal, tax, or technical advice**. Nothing contained herein should be construed as a recommendation to buy, sell, trade, lend, borrow, stake, or engage in any transaction involving cryptocurrencies, tokens, NFTs, or other digital assets.

Any strategies, tools, or techniques discussed, including but not limited to trading, yield farming, MEV mitigation, wallet security, or smart contract interaction are illustrative only. **Readers assume full responsibility and all risks** for any actions taken based on this material, including but not limited to financial loss, security breaches, smart contract failures, liquidation events, or regulatory consequences.

Cryptocurrency and DeFi activities can carry **extreme risk**, including the potential for total loss of principal. Past performance is not indicative of future results. Readers should conduct their own research, consult qualified professionals, and only participate with capital they can afford to lose.

The author and publisher make no warranties—express or implied regarding the completeness, reliability, or suitability of the content. Use of third-party tools, platforms, or services mentioned is at the reader's sole discretion and risk.

By reading this book, you acknowledge and accept these terms in full.

ISBN: 978-0-9966012-7-6 Paperback edition
ISBN: 978-0-9966012-6-9 Hardback edition

Table of Contents

Preface: Why your wallet is the new bank

In 2008, Satoshi Nakamoto offered a simple trade:

Give up the convenience of trusting strangers. Gain the power of verifying everything.

In 2026, AI supercharges that trade.

Your wallet is no longer a leather billfold or a mobile app. It is a sovereign node, a fusion of cryptography, artificial intelligence, and legal engineering that fits in your pocket.

For most of human history, a "bank" was a building with vaults, tellers, and ledgers. You walked in, handed over paper, and trusted strangers to guard your wealth. That model worked, until it didn't.

In 2008, we watched centralized trust collapse. In 2022, we saw $40 billion vanish from FTX overnight. In 2025, the Coinbase breach reminded us that even the most "secure" custodians can leak 70,000 client selfies[1] to the dark web. The lesson is clear: custody is a liability.

Enter the sovereign wallet. It is not a product you buy; it is a capability you activate. A private keypair, encrypted on your device, becomes the root of your financial identity. No middleman can freeze it, seize it, or monetize it without your consent. This is not ideology, it is infrastructure. The same cryptography that secures Bitcoin can now secure your driver's license, your stock certificates, and your AI agent's reputation score.

But sovereignty without intelligence is brittle. This is where AI enters the vault. Your wallet is no longer a dumb keyring; it is a sovereign agent. It watches your spending patterns and whispers, *"You're leaking $2,100 a year on coffee, here's how to cut it."* It scans on-chain yields and says, *"Move $5,000 from checking to Aave's USDC pool with 8.2 % APY, same-day exit and no KYC required."*

It detects phishing before you click, using behavioral biometrics trained only on your device, all while you sip your (now cheaper) coffee.

This book is a practical map, not a manifesto. You will learn:

- **Self-custody without paranoia**: How to generate, back up, and recover keys using hardware wallets, seed phrases, and social recovery, without trusting any single device or person.

---

1 Selfies used to ID users as part of the KYC process.

- **AI-optimized yields**: How to deploy idle capital into battle-tested DeFi, and tokenized treasuries, with AI agents that rebalance, hedge, and alert in real time.

- **Tokenization for everyone**: Trade RWA (real-world assets) for high passive income. Real estate, T-Bills and more via tradable, yield-bearing tokens.

- **Privacy by design**: Use zero-knowledge proofs and selective disclosure to prove "I'm over 21" or "I own this asset" without ever exposing the underlying data.

- **Defensive security** to protect yourself, your systems and your assets from the most determined attacks. With DeFi specific defense.

The bank of the future is not a skyscraper on Wall Street. It is the encrypted enclave in your pocket, running open-source code, guarded by mathematics, and guided by an AI that answers only to you. When you hold your keys, you hold your freedom. When your wallet holds your AI, you hold your edge.

This is not the end of finance. It is the beginning of personal finance, where every individual is their own central bank, and every transaction is a vote for the world they want to live in.

Turn the page.
Your first deposit is knowledge.
Your first withdrawal is control.
Enjoy.

How to Use this book

Achieving sovereign financial freedom is a journey.

And the very first step is understanding just how entwined we all are, or have been in the surveillance and over bearing Matrix of the traditional financial world. Reading this book, will open your eyes and set you on the path to true financial freedom.

And the freedoms unlocked are priceless.

1. Unrestricted Access. Funds move 24/7, globally, without borders or holidays. An Argentine freelancer gets paid in USDC, dodging 100%+ inflation.

2. Censorship resistance means no freezes. Canadian truckers saw banks seize accounts in 2022; Bitcoin holders were untouchable.

3. Inflation hedge. Self-custodied Bitcoin has delivered a compound annual growth rate (CAGR) of over 200% since its first exchange-traded price in late 2009, fiat's silent thief of inflation[2] can't touch it.

But reading is not enough, the magic starts with action, action, action.

---

[2] The pattern is clear, fiat currency is designed to lose value over time. Everything that can't be printed has dramatically outperformed it.

First, don't get overwhelmed! Its easy to be when you see how we are all treated as financial slaves by the system.

Some of the concepts and strategies are very simple, other are more advanced. Likewise the chapters. Some list technologies that are available right now. Others discuss whats coming next.

So treat this book as an overview of what's possible. Pick the strategies you like and start there. You can always bookmark and circle back to others.

Secondly, start slow. I've detailed numerous actions, Sovereignty Fixes[3] you can take. You don't have to do everything on Day 1.

Lastly, if you read something that is confusing, a new concept, term etc, we will dive deeper into most subjects as we move forward. I've added a lot of content, but don't have the space to write in-depth guides for everything. So use this book as a stepping stone and drill deeper into the parts that interest you.

Okay, that it. Ready, set, go to savings and increased and secure financial freedom.

---

3 Use the Index in the End Matter section to find all of them.

Part I: The Sovereign Mindset

The Sovereign Mindset is a philosophy of absolute financial autonomy. It fuses blockchain's decentralization, AI's intelligence, and privacy's armor to break the grip of Big Banks and Big Brother.

This isn't just about making money, it's about owning it completely, free from interference, surveillance, or seizure.

Rejecting Centralized Control

Traditional finance is built on trust in intermediaries. Banks, processors, clearing houses, credit rating agencies. They charge fees, freeze accounts, and track every move. A single "suspicious activity" flag can lock you out.

The Sovereign Mindset rejects this.

Money becomes code: self-custodied, programmable, borderless.

Blockchains are the foundation. Bitcoin, Ethereum, Solana and other cryptocurrencies enable direct, trustless transfers using private keys.

You don't ask permission, you act.

Privacy as Power

Privacy isn't for criminals. It's defense against surveillance capitalism. Big Tech and data brokers harvest transaction data to profile, predict, and control.

The Sovereign Mindset defaults to opacity.

Zero-knowledge proofs verify transactions without exposing details. Privacy coins like Monero, Dash and Zcash hide sender, receiver, and amount.

Privacy chains like Secret Network (a layer 1 built with the Cosmos SDK), Oasis Network, Beam and Grin and others run encrypted smart contracts. Your spending stays yours, un-traceable, un-manipulable, to the degree you want it to be.

You are in control, not a clause on page 30 of the Banks terms and conditions you signed without reading or understanding.

AI as Autonomous Ally

AI turns defense into offense. Decentralized agents built on Fetch.ai, SingularityNET, or local nodes, optimize wealth without centralized oversight. They swap assets on DeFi protocols like Aave, Compound and others, predict dips via on-chain oracles, and rebalance instantly.

Homomorphic encryption[4] lets AI compute on encrypted data, managing funds blindly.

Result: 10–50% yields in stable DeFi environments, versus 0.01% in savings accounts.

The Disciple of Sovereignty

Freedom demands responsibility. "Not your keys, not your crypto" is more than cute phase, its real to you.

You secure your seed phrases, use multi-sig wallets and audit contracts[5] on Etherscan.

AI flags phishing, privacy mixers (Railgun, Tornado successors) break linkability. The risks are yours to manage with no bailouts and no-one else to blame.

The Network Flywheel

Adoption drives value. El Salvador's Bitcoin experiment, MicroStrategy's billions in BTC. Each user strengthens liquidity, oracles, AI models. This is Metcalfe's Law in action: more sovereigns = a richer ecosystem.

The Sovereign Mindset isn't ideology, it's engineering.

---

[4] Homomorphic encryption = is a method of encoding data that allows computations to be performed on the encrypted data without needing to decrypt it first.

[5] Very easy to do a basic safety check (5–10 minutes).

It restricts gatekeepers, not users.

It delivers control, efficiency, and superior returns.

In a world of financial predation, sovereignty isn't optional.

It's survival.

Chapter 1 - The Death of Third-Party Trust

"Not your keys, not your crypto."
Every Bitcoin maximalist since 2013

"Not your data, not your future."
You, 2026

The Night your Bank Forgot You

It was 2:14 a.m. on a Tuesday in October 2024 when 4.2 million Americans discovered their life savings had been *paused*.

Not stolen.
Not seized.
PAUSED.

A routine software upgrade at one of the largest U.S. custodian banks triggered a cascading failure in the ACH network. For 36 hours, direct deposits vanished, debit cards were declined, and payroll systems showed $0.00 balances. The cascading failure caused backups in the network shared with numerous other banks, causing them to queue transactions as well. The result was panic for many regular bank customers.

Meanwhile the bank that started posted a pastel graphic on its Twitter (X) account:

"We're working hard to restore access. Thank you for your patience."

No cyberattack was involved, as many had believed, it was purely a technical error.

Meanwhile, in early March 2025, Yotta, a popular U.S. fintech savings app with gamified high-yield accounts suddenly froze access to customer funds due to a technical dispute and backend glitch involving its partner bank.

The issue arose from a collapse in the third-party middleware provider Synapse Brokerage, which handled transaction routing between Yotta and Evolve Bank & Trust. A software integration failure caused pending deposits and withdrawals to get stuck in limbo, effectively freezing 150,000 users' accounts
with over $100 million in total funds locked. Some users couldn't access even small balances for daily expenses, leading to overdrafts and bounced payments.

Resolution took 10–14 days after Yotta sued Evolve for "withholding deposits," with the FDIC stepping in to audit. These and many other similar events were not edge cases. They were features of a financial system built on third-party trust that exposes how fintechs' reliance on layered tech stacks can amplify glitches into widespread freezes.

By 2026, the pause button has become the ultimate power tool of the legacy stack. A single line of code, executed by a faceless risk engine, can freeze your rent money, your grocery budget, your child's tuition.

And the worst part?

You agreed to it in paragraph 47 of the Terms of Service you clicked "accept" on in 2019.

To be clear, this chapter is not about fear. It's about diagnosis.

We will autopsy the three invisible trust layers you still hand over every time you tap your phone to pay for coffee.

Then we'll hand you the scalpel to cut out the problems in your financial life.

Layer 1: The Bank as Custodian of Value

In 2008, Lehman Brothers collapsed. $600B in client assets was "missing". Fractional reserve banking was exposed.

In 2022, Celsius Network, paused withdrawals. The result was CeFi lending imploded.

In 2023, during the Silicon Valley Bank (SVB) bank run, the FDIC stepped in AFTER $42B had been withdrawn (25% of total deposits) and clients faced days of "frozen deposits". Everyone found out that Deposit Insurance is reactive and many were totally under insured. In the end, taxpayer funds bailed out depositors, but trust in the system was further eroded.

In 2024, the ACH system was "paused" and funds were " unavailable" due to a failed software upgrade at Bank of America (BoA). Many found out that even insured money can be inaccessible for days.

The Lie & Truth

The Lie of the banking system is "Your money is safe in a regulated bank".

The Truth is your money is safe until a regulator changes the rules.

In 2025, the Basel IV capital rules quietly reclassified stablecoins as "high-risk assets." Overnight, 47 regional banks off-boarded their crypto-native clients.
No appeal.
No grandfather clause.
Just an email: *"We can no longer service your account."*

Sovereignty Fix: Proof of Custody

Move value to bearer instruments you control.

Proof of custody = verifiable evidence that a custodian, in this case you, controls the private keys to specific bitcoin addresses without exposing them.

Start with $1000 in Bitcoin. The goal is not speculation, it's proof of custody, real-time, transparent, and trust-minimized.

Add some stablecoins and you are set to make payments directly, engage in yield bearing activities via DeFi and buy tokens via decentralized exchanges. All without middle men, and without gatekeepers who can shut you out and without extra fees.

Welcome to the start of your financial freedom.

Layer 2: The App as custodian of Access

Open your phone. Count the finance apps.
Average American in 2025 has 7.

- Banking app
- Investment app
- Crypto exchange app
- Payments app
- Tax app
- Credit score app
- Budget app

And each one is a single point of failure.

A few examples to illustrate the point.

In Jan, 2021, Robinhood halted trading in GameStop Corp (GME) when retail traders caused a short squeeze driving the stock to over $500 per share and costing hedge funds who were shorting, massive losses.

Robinhood, restricted trading on GameStop and several other stocks by halting the ability of retail investors to place buy orders, although sell orders and existing positions could be closed out.

Ultimately, Robinhood's trading halt lasted from January 28 until partial lifting of purchase restrictions by January 30 or 31, about 2-3 days total.

In 2023, another notable case emerged involving a UK freelancer who was locked out of their PayPal accounts for about six months.

The incident began when PayPal froze the freelancer's business account following an unusual spike in orders, which triggered the platform's risk controls.

Although the freelancer provided requested documentation and initially seemed to resolve the issue, their funds were held for 180 days as per PayPal's policy, leading to significant challenges in accessing their money.

This is not an isolated incident either.

There have been multiple similar cases involving PayPal where freelancers and small business users have faced sudden account restrictions or freezes, often with little notice or clear explanation.

Common experiences include:

- Accounts being locked or restricted after unusual transaction activity or disputes, with PayPal requesting excessive documentation for verification.

- Funds placed on hold for up to 180 days, severely impacting cash flow for individuals dependent on timely payments.

- Permanent limitations or closures of accounts due to perceived "risk" or "policy violations," sometimes without clear recourse or proper customer support engagement.

- Threats of collections or negative balances due to PayPal crediting disputed or reversed funds, even when the user has not been at fault.

In May 2024, (publicized in 2025) SogoTrade, an online brokerage, announced a data breach exposing customer names, financial account numbers, social security numbers, and tax IDs. The breach gave hackers ample information to facilitate phishing and fraud against clients.

In all of these cases, financial apps have been at fault for losing customer data, for locking accounts and pausing trading, locking users out.

The Lie & Truth

All financial apps are potentially open to being attacked or restricting users access to their funds.

Even adding two-factor authentication (2FA) doesn't lessen the downside. While I'm a big fan of 2FA on all websites and social media accounts I regularly use, the fact remains, the 2FA protects the app, not you. If the app decides you are a risk, your 2FA code is just a longer password to nowhere.

Sovereignty Fix: Proof of Access

Consolidate into a non-custodial wallet with hardware signing.

One seed phrase beats seven logins any day.

Layer 3: The Cloud as custodian of Data

Every transaction you make is a data exhaust pipe feeding:

- Plaid (connects 12,000+ banks)
- Yodlee (owned by Envestnet)
- Google Analytics / Firebase
- AWS / Azure billing logs
- And more

In 2025, the average DeFi user generates 1.2 GB of on-chain + off-chain behavioral data per year. That data is sliced, packaged, and sold to:

- Advertisers ("Earn 18% APY!" push notifications)
- Insurers (raise your premium because you hold volatile assets)

- Governments (tax audits triggered by “irregular yield patterns”)

Case Study: The 2025 Texas DAO Raid

A privacy-focused DAO in Austin used Tornado Cash to pool member funds for public goods. Chainalysis flagged the DAO's Tornado Cash smart contract.

The IRS issued 312 John Doe summons to centralized crypto on/off ramps to obtain information on users interacting with Tornado Cash and related contracts.

The Result: 47 members doxxed, $2.1M in retroactive taxes.

Sovereignty Fix

Route data through zero-knowledge mixers and decentralized identity (e.g., zk-proof of residency without revealing address).

Unlike traditional crypto mixers that pool and shuffle coins from multiple users to obscure transaction trails, zero-knowledge mixers leverage zero-knowledge proofs to verify the validity of transactions without revealing any sensitive details such as sender, recipient, or transaction amount.

In practice, a zero-knowledge mixer works by allowing a user to deposit funds into a smart contract along with a cryptographic "commitment."

Later, the user or recipient generates a zero-knowledge proof that they know a secret related to the deposit, enabling them to withdraw the funds independently without linking the withdrawal back to the deposit. This process breaks the on-chain link between sending and receiving addresses completely, providing stronger privacy guarantees.

The Trust Collapse Timeline (2008 - 2026)

2008 - The Global Financial Crisis
- the Trust layer destroyed = Banks
- Sovereign strategy = The Bitcoin whitepaper

2103 - Mt.Gox hack
- Trust layer destroyed = Centralized Exchange
- Sovereign strategy = Self cold storage

2017 - ICO mania/ hype
- Trust layer destroyed = Trust in Token launches -
- Sovereign strategy = Due diligence matters

2020 - the DeFi Summer
- Trust layer destroyed = CeFi yields
- Sovereign strategy = Self custody

2022 - Terra/ Luna
- Trust layer destroyed = Algorithmic stablecoins

- Sovereign strategy = Only ever collateralized DeFi

2023 - FTX
- Trust layer destroyed = Algorithmic stablecoins
- Sovereign strategy = Only ever collateralized DeFi

2024 - ACH Outage
- Trust layer destroyed = Payment rails
- Sovereign strategy = Stablecoin payments

2026 - Your turn now
- Trust layer destroyed = All in this chapter
- Your sovereign strategy = Sovereign wallet

Your First Act of Sovereignty

Right now, open your phone's Notes app and write:
"I control my keys. I control my future."

Screenshot it. Set it as your lock screen.
That sentence is worth more than the $ you paid for this book.

Because the moment you *believe* it, the game changes.

The banks will still send pastel graphics.

The apps will still freeze.

The regulators will still draw red lines.

But you?

You'll be on the other side of the moat.

Chapter 2 - Your Data, Your Money, Your Rules

"If you're not paying for the product, you are the product."
Old Internet saying

"If you're paying with dollars, you're still the product."
You, after reading this chapter

The Invisible Auction Happening Right Now

Every time you buy a $4.29 latte with Apple Pay, seven companies place a bid on the metadata of that transaction before the barista hands you the cup.

1. Visa – Interchange fee + risk score
2. Plaid – Connected to your bank for "budgeting insights"
3. Starbucks – Loyalty points + purchase graph
4. Google – Location ping + ad ID
5. Equifax – Credit header update
6. Chainalysis – If you ever bridged that latte money from crypto

Total time: 0.8 seconds.

Total value extracted from you: $0.11 in fees + $1.40 in future ad targeting (lifetime value).
Your cut: 0.00.

This is not a conspiracy. It's a feature of the legacy financial stack.

And it's about to get worse with ChatGPT (and soon others AI's) adding ads to their platforms.

The $2 Trillion Surveillance Economy (2026 Edition)

Unlike traditional capitalism, surveillance capitalism treats human experience as a raw material. Free services (e.g., Gmail, Maps, your social media apps) lure users into data generation, which is commodified for ad targeting and/or sold to data brokers, who in turn sell personal data to almost anyone who will pay for it.

Google earns over $300 billion from its Ads and Android telemetry tracking users everywhere extracting vast amounts of personal user data—often without explicit meaningful consent—to predict and influence behavior for profit.

Meta earns over $190 billion from Facebook, Instagram & WhatApp and Messenger fuels hyper-targeted advertising. This accounts for over 98% of their total revenue.

Amazon earns approximately $50 billion from its advertising services and partnerships with Roku and Netflix and Amazon Pay fees.

While Apple earns relatively little from its ad services, approximately $6 billion annually, it is more privacy focussed than its tech peers. It still extracts over $5 billion from Apple Pay and Apple Card transaction fees.

Plaid & Yodlee earn over $1.2 billion via connecting users to over 12,000 bank connections.

The biggest player in the surveillance economy is the wild west data broker industry. Thousands of firms collecting user data, mostly unregulated and with almost no consent, selling this data to anyone who will pay for it. Combined revenues over $330 billion in 2025 growing at approximately 7-8% CAGR incentive their behavior.

Additionally data brokers commonly buy information from third parties that track your browsing activities using tracking cookies. In some cases data brokers also place cookies on your browser to provide their clients with the ability to target you with ads across the web. Likewise they buy information related to your purchasing habits and which subscriptions you paid for.

This fuels targeted advertising, risk assessment, and decision-making, often drawing criticism for privacy invasions.

The Data Broker Problem

The data broker industry harms consumers in multiple ways with their collection, aggregation and sale of personal information. These effects are well-documented in government reports (FTC, GAO, CFPB), academic studies, and consumer advocacy research.

1. **Privacy Erosion & Loss of Control**

Brokers compile 1,000+ data points per person (e.g., income, health conditions, political views, sexual orientation, location history) from public records, online tracking, loyalty programs, and app data.

Consumers cannot see, correct[6] or even delete their profiles. Although they have limited options to request brokers not sell their data, many don't comply and add users back again after new data is collected.

The FTC in a 2023 study concluded that 74% of Americans feel they have no control over their data. They are correct, they don't.

And even worse a lot of sensitive data is sold without the consumers knowledge including pregnancy, depression, sexual orientation, religious affiliation and more.

---

6 A GAO study in 2022 showed 43% of data broker profiles contained inaccurate data.

The real world impact of this is stalking, doxxing and in many cases blackmail (e.g. location data in domestic abuse cases).

2. Discrimination & Unfair treatment

Data is used for risk scoring in lending, insurance, hiring and housing.

Harmful outcomes can include discriminatory effects[7] in;

Credit & loans with "digital redlining" with Zip codes and growing history resulting in being charged higher interest rates.

Insurance companies can use health inferences from pharmacy purchases resulting in either denied coverage or higher premiums.

In hiring, companies use "people analytics" firms to score candidates on their social media activity, resulting in cases of bias against individuals and even protected classes or people. And candidates have no idea this occurs.

In housing landlords use "eviction predictions" to deny rentals to lower-income or in case. Minority applicants.

There are numerous examples of all of the above in cases studies and all of this is widely known, yet few new regulations have been put in place to deal with the problem.

---

[7] Research shows 1 in 5 loan denials is inflated by non-FCRA data.

Case in point, in a 2024 CFPB Report, data brokers were found to enable algorithmic discrimination violating Fair Credit Reporting Act (FCRA).

3. Financial Fraud and Identity Theft

Data brokers sell full package identity packages tat include mothers maiden name, date-of-birth and SSNs.

The consequences of this is with your data held in countless numbers of firms systems hackers breach companies all the time and flood personal private data onto dark-web forums. Dark-web prices for a full identity package, source from a dat broker, run from $1000 to $2000 each for complete US based identity kit.

The result is identity theft is a $10.3 billion problem that wastes countless hours and frustration for the victims as they struggle to rebuild their lives after an identity theft attack with their credit often trashed.

Case in point, in 2017 Equifax, one of the largest credit bureaus was hacked and 147 million had their personal private data exposed, data that was originally collected by a "legitimate brokerage".

4. Price Gouging & Predatory Marketing

Brokers segment consumers into "vulnerable" tiers (eg.e the elderly, recent divorcees, low-income) and sell that data to pay day lenders, for-profit collages, insurance firms, etc.

Pay day lenders then target " financially fragile" profiles with exorbitant fees.

For-profit collages buy leads of "opportunity seekers" and target them with programs and associated costs they otherwise don't need and with little value in the real world.

And due to "dynamic pricing" the same product end up costing the vulnerable more if their data show desperation.

Case in point, a Princeton study in 2021 showed online ads for loans with higher APRs for older user and blah people, all based on data broker obtained information.

Sovereignty Fix to the data broker problem

Use privacy focussed tools like brokerage data removal firms DeleteMe, Optery, Incogni, etc,, to remove your profiles from data brokers. Its a long process, but this cuts out a lot of your personal data from being sold.

Stop using Google as a search engine! Use privacy search like DuckDuckGo, Brave Search and Mojeek. And yes, they work just as well as Google does.

Use fake date of birth information on social media sites[8]

Use privacy focused emails like Protonmail. Ditch your gmail account!

[8] Note, this may violate their terms of service but the risk of them sharing your real data needs to be balanced.

The Sovereign Stack: 3 Layers to Freedom

Layer 1 - Identity

- Old way = KYV + selfie
- Sovereign strategy = zk-passport (prove without showing who you are)

Layer 2 - Payments

- Old way = 3% card fees + your data sold
- Sovereign strategy = USDC + Lightning network ($0.01)

Layer 3 - Intelligence

- Old way = Bank AI world for them
- Sovereign strategy = Your AI agent works for you

Layer 1: Reclaim Your Identity (with no selfies involved)

The KYC Trap

Exchanges demand:

- Government ID
- A selfie with todays date
- In some cases a utility bill

Then they store it all in the cloud!

In the 2025 Coinbase breach [9], 67k selfies were leaked resulting in a claimed $180 million drained via deepfakes and phishing attacks, although the true extend of the damage is unclear.

Sovereignty Fix - Zero-Knowledge Proofs

Prove your over 18, a US resident and not sanctioned all without revealing your name.

Tools:

- Use apps like ZKPassport.id or Self (iOS/Android)—scan your passport NFC, create proofs for attributes like age/citizenship.
- Or if an advanced user, use a secure hardware wallet like a Keystone Wallet with SpruceID.
- Generate a zk-passport.
- Use in DefFi, DAO's etc, no more KYC.

If you are asking what exactly is a ZK-passport, lets dive in.

A ZK-Passport (or zk-passport) is an emerging privacy-preserving digital identity tool built on zero-knowledge proofs (ZKPs). It allows users to verify specific attributes from a government-issued document (like a biometric passport or national ID) without revealing the full details. It transforms a physical ID into a reusable, selective-disclosure

9 An insider-driven data incident where overseas contractors were bribed into leaking sensitive user data.

credential, primarily for Web3, decentralized applications (dApps), and online services.

With a zk-passport no personal info leaves your device; only chosen attributes (e.g., "over 18") are proven. It complies with standards like ICAO 9303 for electronic passports.

Examples of zk-passports include the zkpassport.id app which supports over 120 countries. The Rarimo ZK Passport focusses on web3 integrations with on-line registries and Self Project, Open Passport built on Ethereum.

The benefits of a zk-passport are many, a one-time scan, reusable proofs and no data storage by third parties reducing the risk of a data breach.

As of 2025, apps like Self (iOS/Android) have thousands of users for Web3 logins. Integrations with Aztec, Wormhole, and PayPal Ventures-backed projects signal growth in AI/DeFi.

Challenges include NFC hardware limits and regulatory hurdles, but proofs are fast (seconds on mobiles) and cost-effective (~$0.01 to 0.10 per verification).

This is an emerging space. Pilots and integrations are accelerating due to regulatory pressure (e.g., MiCA in EU, AMLD6) and privacy demands. In particular CEXs are requited to comply with AML/KYC regulations more and more will accept zk-passports.
Expect CEX pilots by 2026 as EU's eIDAS 2.0 mandates privacy tech. And while many will avoid centralized

exchanges, many decentralized exchanges lack fiat on/off ramps if required[10].

In essence, ZK-Passports bridge physical-world trust with digital privacy, making "prove it without showing it" a reality for everything from crypto wallets to global travel.

Layer 2: Reclaim Your Payments (No Fees)

You pay $1,200/year in hidden card fees on $40k spend.

This is a realistic, data-backed estimate of how much the average U.S. consumer indirectly pays in credit card processing fees when spending $40,000 annually on cards. You don't see a line item, but merchants pass these costs to you via higher prices, whether you pay with cash, debit, or credit.

Thats $100 baked into the price, even if you pay with cash! You pay this indirectly because merchants raise prices to cover fees[11].

Studies show ~70 to 100% of swipe fees are passed to consumers (Federal Reserve, 2023).

It's economics. The more you spend on plastic, the more you subsidize the card industry.

---

10 See Chapter 9 for more on fiat off-ramps. There are many.

11 FYI try and avoid Avoid Amex/Diners as they charge merchants 3.5–4.0%

Sovereignty Fix - Payments

1. Install the Strike app, a mobile-first Bitcoin payments platform developed by Zap Solutions, Inc.

Strike leverages the Bitcoin Lightning Network (a layer-2 scaling solution) to enable instant, low-cost global transfers.

Unlike traditional crypto exchanges, Strike acts more like a digital wallet and remittance service, think Venmo or Cash App, but powered by Bitcoin for borderless, fee-minimal transactions. Its tagline: "Send cash, receive Bitcoin" (or vice versa), making it ideal for remittances, micropayments, and everyday spending.

2. Send $100 USDT to a friend
3. See it arrive in 2 seconds.
4. Replace one bill this month.

Layer 3: Reclaim Your Intelligence with Your Own IA Agent.

Their AI vs Your AI

Theirs = predicts overdraft -> sells $39 fee
Yours = Finds 12% to 15% yield -> earns you $600 (or more)

Theirs = nudges high-fee funds
Yours = auto-rebalances weekly

Theirs = works for the bank
Yours = works for you

Why 12 to 15% APY Exists in DeFi

Just reading the example above I'm sure some will see 12% to 15% APY and think, no way!

Well actually this is correct and let me explain why.

That 15% yield on offer is the time premium on the slowness of the traditional banking system.

At first glance, 15% APY on USDC or USDT looks like a red flag. Professional hedge funds, with teams of PhDs and nine-figure AUM, routinely *underperform* that benchmark after fees. If the smartest money on Earth can't clear 15% net, how can a DeFi app paying retail depositors that much possibly be legit?

The answer is pure market mechanics, and a structural bottleneck that TradFi can't fix.

Let's break it down simply. Crypto markets are 24/7 and brutally volatile. During chaos, the same asset can trade at wildly different prices across exchanges.

A market maker with $10 million in capital sees a $100 million arbitrage opportunity. They want in, but they're stuck. They need $90 million *right now*. Banks won't lend for "magic internet money" on a Friday night, and besides everyone's asleep.

Even if they would, wiring cash, converting to USDC, and moving it to the exchange takes 48–72 hours. By then, the trade's gone.

So what do pros do? They borrow instantly on-chain from protocols like Aave, Morpho, or Maple. They'll happily pay 30–50% APY because their expected return is *way* higher. Borrow $90 million at 40% for one week, execute the trade in minutes, repay the loan, and walk away with a 39%+ return in hours. That's not gambling, its pure math.

This is where your 15% comes from. The yield flows downstream:

- Arbitrageurs pay 40–100%+ APY to capture inefficiencies
- Protocols take a small cut (3–10%)
- The rest goes to passive lenders like you and me who provide liquidity in DeFi

So that 15% isn't conjured out of thin air. It's the time premium on capital that can deploy in 10 seconds instead of 72 hours.

Crypto needs instant liquidity. Traditional finance can't provide it. That gap, this structural inefficiency, is the yield.

Sovereignty Fix: No Code Needed

Your 3 step Financial Co-Pilot

1. Your bank app

- Export transactions as CSV (Transactions, download , CSV)
- Time = 30 seconds

2. Upload to Encrypted Vault.
- Go to skiff.com (free, end-trend encrypted)
- Sign up with email
- Create a private drive, name it finances
- Drag and drop your bank transactions CSV file (its encrypted and secure)

3. Go to finpilot.ai and sign up.
- upload the CSV from Skiff
- Tap "run Co-pilot"
- AI output in chat "Your leaking $2100/ year on coffee", "Move $5k to Aave USDC and earn $410/ year at 8.2%" "Next step, want me to draft a transfer?"

4. No data sold, no ads.

5. Set bank to auto-export CSV weekly via email.
- Skiff can auto import from email
- Finpilot can run weekly reports you get a push notification "weekly financial health report"

6. You save $1000+ / in savings - no code, no hassle.

All possible because you drew a line in the sand in 2026.

Part II: The AI-Powered Wallet

"When AI agents are built on crypto rails, new possibilities emerge. Transactions become programmable, and crypto complexity gets abstracted away."
privy.io

Chapter 3 - Anatomy of a 2026 Sovereign Wallet

"The sovereign individual is the person who controls their own keys, their own identity, and their own data. The sovereign wallet is the tool that makes this possible."

Balaji S. Srinivasan, The Network State conference keynote, Amsterdam, 2023

AI-powered sovereign wallets represent the next evolution: intelligent, adaptive systems that not only store credentials but also anticipate user needs, enhance security through machine learning, and facilitate seamless interactions in a multi-chain, agentic world.

These wallets transform passive storage into proactive guardianship, where AI acts as a smart assistant, analyzing patterns, mitigating threats, and optimizing disclosures while upholding the sovereignty principle, all with no central authority and no data silos waiting to get hacked.

This chapter explores the fusion of AI and SSI wallets, tracing their technological foundations, practical implementations, benefits, challenges, and future trajectory. These innovations are not mere hypotheticals; they are reshaping finance, governance, and social interactions.

Foundations

Self-Sovereign Identity (SSI)[12], emerged in the mid-2010s as a response to the limitations of federated identity models, where users rely on providers like OAuth for authentication.

Digital wallets serve as the user interface for SSI. Unlike traditional crypto wallets (e.g., MetaMask for Ethereum), sovereign wallets are multi-purpose repositories. Tamper-proof digital equivalents of diplomas, passports, or medical records.

Users "present" these credentials to verifiers (e.g. a bank or employer) via zero-knowledge proofs (ZKPs), proving attributes like "over 18" without exposing extraneous details.

Standards from the World Wide Web Consortium (W3C), such as DID and VC specifications, ensure interoperability, while frameworks like the European Self-Sovereign Identity Framework (ESSIF) integrate SSI with regulations like eIDAS.

AI enters this ecosystem as the "power layer." Machine learning algorithms, powered by neural networks and large language models (LLMs), augment wallet functionality in three primary ways:

---

12 Self-Sovereign Identity (SSI) turns the traditional identity model on its head. Instead of governments or issuing corporations as the root of trust, you hold verifiable credentials in your sovereign wallet, cryptographically prove attributes about yourself (age, citizenship, accreditation, etc.) without revealing anything else, and no central party can revoke or track them."

- perception (analyzing user behavior and external data),
- cognition (decision-making and automation),
- action (executing secure interactions).

Yet, the true innovation lies in autonomy. AI empowers wallets to evolve from reactive tools to proactive entities, learning from user interactions to refine privacy policies or automate compliance checks. As one X post from a Web3 architect notes, "AI doesn't need banks, it needs rails."

This agentic shift blurs lines between human and machine identities, heralding an "intelligent economy" where wallets aren't just vaults—they're vigilant stewards.

Case Studies: AI Sovereign Wallets in Action

Real-world deployments illustrate the transformative potential. Consider the SpruceID platform that powers SSI for governments and enterprises.

In partnership with California's DMV, Spruce's wallet issues mobile driver's licenses (mDLs) verified by TSA, using AI to match live biometrics against stored hashes, reducing verification time by 80% while preventing deepfake fraud.

In finance, Dock Wallet exemplifies DeFi integration.

Users store verifiable credential (VC)[13] like accredited investor status, with AI optimizing disclosures for platforms like Aave. A 2025 pilot with Naturellica allowed job applicants to prove Jira certifications via ZKPs, where AI curated proofs from educational VC's, boosting hiring efficiency by 40%.

For AI agents, KiteAI stands out. KiteAI equips agents with sovereign wallets for on-chain reputation building and verifying actions like token swaps while auditing for biases.

In one deployment, agents autonomously staked user funds in Cosmos pools, earning 8.2% APY, with AI ensuring unlinkable pseudonyms for privacy.

These cases demonstrate scalability. From individual verifications to ecosystem-wide trust, AI amplifies SSI's reach without eroding control.

Conclusion: Towards an Intelligent, Sovereign Future.

AI-powered sovereign wallets are not just technological artifacts, they are blueprints for a reimagined digital social contract. By merging blockchain's immutability with AI's foresight, these tools empower users to navigate an agentic world with confidence, verifying credentials for a loan,

[13] A Verifiable Credential is a tamper-proof, cryptographically signed digital certificate that proves something about you (or your wallet) without needing to trust a central party every time.

delegating tasks to AI proxies, or proving humanity in DAO votes, all while retaining control.

As we stand now, the horizon gleams with possibility. Sovereign wallets, infused with AI, promise a future where identity is not a commodity but a superpower, private, portable, and profoundly human.

Chapter 4 - AI Agents That Pay Your Bills

"The future of money is not a bank account. It's a sovereign wallet with an AI agent that never sleeps, never forgets, and never asks for permission."
The Sovereign Wallet, 2025

We are entering a new phase of the digital economy with the rise in use of smart AI agentic agents. However, I believe most people are underestimating the impact agentic agent workflows will have. They envision humans using agents to book hotels, flights and do everyday work tasks for them. And while that will be a big part of the early adoption, the real growth will be in agent to agent transactions. They will result in true frictionless, millisecond transactions doing so many tasks, we haven't even thought about yet.

The End of Manual Money

You wake up. Your phone lights up with a simple message:

"Rent paid. $2,400 sent. Gas bill due in 3 days, paid early, saved you $12."

You didn't open an app.

You didn't log in.

You didn't even think about it.

Your wallet did it, quietly, safely, and on your terms. This isn't a dream.

In 2025, regular people are already using AI-powered sovereign wallets to pay rent or their mortgages, utilities, subscriptions, and even taxes automatically.

And they're doing it without giving up control of their money.

This chapter is for you, the person who wants financial peace of mind without needing a finance degree. We'll walk through:

- How we got here (from cash to apps to AI wallets)
- How your wallet can now pay your bills for you
- Real-life examples of people saving thousands
- A simple 15-minute setup (no tech skills needed)
- Why now is the best time to switch—and how it pays off

By the end, you'll see your wallet not as a place to store money, but as a smart, loyal assistant that works for you 24/7.

A Brief History of Money (and Why We're Done with Banks)

Let's go back in time, just far enough to see how we got stuck, and how we're finally getting free.

Pre-1900
= Cash, gold, barter
= Hard to carry, easy to steal

1900–1980
= Checks, bank tellers
= Slow, paperwork, bank hours

1980–2000
= Credit cards, ATMs
= Convenient, but you paid 18% interest

2000–2024
= Online banking, Venmo, PayPal
= Fast, but your data was sold, accounts frozen

2025–2026 +
= Crypto, DeFi, AI wallets
= **Freedom**—you control your money

The Turning Points

- **2008 Financial Crisis**: Banks failed. Millions lost homes. Trust collapsed.

- **2009 Bitcoin**: A new idea—"Not your keys, not your money."
- **2021 DeFi Summer**: People earned 5–10% on savings *without banks*.
- **2022 FTX Collapse**: $8 billion vanished. Lesson: Custody = Risk.
- **2023 AI Boom**: ChatGPT showed AI could *understand* and *act*.
- **2024 Mobile Driver's Licenses**: Governments issued digital IDs you control.
- **2025 Sovereign Wallets**: AI + crypto + legal IDs = your money, your rules.

We're now at the tipping point.

The tools exist.

The trust is gone.

The future is here.

Your Wallet is Smarter than your Bank

Forget leather wallets. Forget bank apps with 17 menus. Your sovereign wallet is a secure app on your phone, backed by a small hardware device (like a USB key). It holds:

- Your money (in Bitcoin, USDC, or dollars)
- Your ID (driver's license, proof of address)
- Your rules ("Pay rent on the 1st, never late")

- An AI agent that follows your rules

So lets talk about AI wallet agents for a bit. Think of them like a smart wallet personal assistant who works for you. Kind of like a super-smart SIRI, but for your money.

You tell this agent:

"Pay my rent $2,400 every 1st. Only to my landlord. Save me money if you can." From then on, the AI:

- Watches the calendar
- Checks your balance
- Verifies the bill is real (using a digital "stamp" from your landlord)
- Pays on time (or early, if there's a discount)
- Tells you: "Done. Saved $72 this year."

You get no spam. None of your data is sold. And no one else touches your money.

And that is priceless.

Real Savings

Sarah, 32, Teacher, Austin

- Old way: Forgot electric bill → $35 late fee
- New way: AI paid early → saved $12/month (pay-on-time discount)
- Potential yearly savings: $420 (no more late fees) + $122 discount = no stress

And pay-on-time discounts for consumers are most common in insurance, utilities, telecommunications, credit services, and subscription-based industries.

George, 28, Freelancer, NYC

- Old way: Missed quarterly taxes → $800 penalty
- New way: AI filed and paid from earnings
- Saved: $3,200 in potential penalties + interest

Mike, 45, Landlord, Miami

- Old way: Tenants paid late 40% of the time
- New way: AI pays on the 28th (with 3% discount) = no more late payments, and fees from collecting
- His gain: $1,200/year per tenant in staff fees chasing up late payments.

These aren't tech geniuses. They are like you and me. They just took action and added a smart wallet AI agent to make payments on time and avoided late fees.

How It Works (In Plain English)

Hardware Wallet
= Keeps your money 100% safe
= Acts like a vault key

Sovereign Wallet app
= Your control center

= the Tria AI app

The Tria AI app, part of a self-custodial neobank platform called Tria, supports making payments. It enables users to spend, trade, and pay bills seamlessly across more than 100 blockchains with no gas fees or custodians.

Digital ID[14]
= Proves it's you
= Enables Ai-optimized Bill Pay for early discounts and it's fraud proof

As of November 5, 2025:

- 14 states have active, live mDL programs (full issuance and use, often TSA-compatible).
- 8+ states are launching in 2025 or early 2026.
- Total projected by end of 2025: 22 states (covering approx. 50% of the US population).
- And currently over 5 million mDLs issued nationwide and growing daily.
- Plus all active programs support federal use (e.g. TSA airports) via DHS waivers. This means seamless payments at federal facilities.

For setup in a supported state, start with your DMV app and a Keystone wallet.

---

14 Not required for all payments. More details in a later chapter.

Part III: Money Without Middlemen

Chapter 5 - Self Custody Without the Panic

Take Control of Your Crypto. Calmly, Safely, and Step by Step

You've probably heard the saying in crypto: "*Not your keys, not your coins.*"

It sounds dramatic, but it's the quiet truth behind every horror story of lost fortunes. This chapter is for everyone who wants to own their money without the heart-pounding fear of "What if I mess this up?"

We'll walk through why millions still leave their crypto on exchanges, what happens when things go wrong, and how you can move to self-custody, the real ownership of your digital wealth, with confidence, not panic.

Think of self-custody as moving your cash from a bank's vault to a safe in your own home. The bank might be convenient, but you're trusting someone else with the combination.

When you hold your own keys, you decide who opens the door and no one else can. The good news? You don't need to be a tech wizard. With the right tools and a little guidance, self-custody is as routine as locking your front door.

Why People Still Use Exchanges (And Why it CAN be Risky)

Let's be honest, centralized exchanges like Coinbase, Binance, or Kraken are incredibly convenient. You sign up with an email, link a bank account, buy Bitcoin or Ethereum in seconds, and watch it sit there.

No confusing wallets. No seed phrases to remember. No worry about losing access. For many, it feels just like online banking, only with crypto. And for small amounts, like $100 to test the waters, that's fine.

But here's the catch: when your crypto lives on an exchange, you don't truly own it.
You're lending it to the platform.
They hold the private keys.
You're a creditor, not an owner.

That's why, during the FTX collapse in 2022, over eight billion dollars vanished overnight. People logged in to find their life savings labeled "unavailable." The same thing happened with smaller platforms like Celsius and Voyager. Even big, trusted names can freeze accounts during market crashes, regulatory probes, or internal failures.

Then there's the quieter danger: hacks and data leaks.

In 2025 alone, the Coinbase breach exposed selfies, addresses, and account balances of nearly 70,000 users. While no crypto was stolen directly, scammers now had perfect targets for phishing, "Click here to secure your funds." One wrong move, and your money is gone.

Exchanges are also prime targets for nation-state hackers. When they get hit, your assets are in the crossfire.

I was nearly a victim of a centralized exchange hack awhile back. I set up an email account to access an exchange, and forgot to add 2FA to the email. Somehow a hacker got into my email, and managed to change my email and password on the exchange. If I didn't have 2FA on my exchange account they could have emptied my account with no recourse. And there would be nothing I could do to recover the funds. Fortunately I'm fairly cybersecurity savvy and undid the damage quickly. However, I was locked out of my own exchange account for nearly 2 weeks while I "proved my identity" again.

And incase you think I'm exaggerating the danger, in just the first half of 2025, centralized crypto exchanges have experienced about $1.88 billion in losses from 11 major hacking incidents.

Numerous reports have concluded centralized crypto exchanges (CEXs) remain highly vulnerable to hacks, with most major breaches involving compromised hot wallets, weak authentication systems, and poor access controls. And with hack detection times around 68 hours there is more than plenty of time for hacks to move crypto and hide tracks.

The final risk with centralized exchanges is you lose control.

Governments can pressure exchanges to freeze funds. A mistaken identity match, a tax audit, or a new regulation can lock you out with no appeal. You're not in charge, the platform is.

The Power of Self-Custody: You Are The Bank

Self-custody flips the script. You generate your own private keys. You store them. You decide when and how to spend.

No one can freeze your Bitcoin because you said the wrong thing online. No one can seize your Ethereum because of a new law. This is financial sovereignty, the same freedom people sought when they first bought gold or hid cash under the mattress, now updated for the digital age.

But let's be real, the idea of managing your own keys can feel overwhelming:

- What if you lose your phone?
- What if you forget a password?
- What if you accidentally send money to the wrong address?

These are valid fears. The good news is that modern self-custody tools are designed for humans, not hackers or geniuses.
They come with backups, recovery options, and safeguards that make mistakes nearly impossible, if you follow a few simple rules.

Self-custody isn't about going it alone. It's about choosing who you trust and how much.

You're not replacing the bank with chaos. You're replacing it with control and calm.

Self-Custody Options: From Simple to Fortress

There's no one-size-fits-all. The right setup depends on how much crypto you have, how often you use it, and how much peace of mind you want.

Here are the main options, explained plainly.

Mobile Browser Wallets

These are free apps that you can install on your phone or laptop. Among the most popular are Metamask, Trust Wallet, Exodus and Phantom Wallet.

You download the app, create a wallet, and write down a 12 or 24 word seed phrase on paper. This phrase acts as a master key. Anyone with it can access your funds, so make a copy and store them safely in separate places.

- Pros = easy, free and fast access if you want to trade.
- Cons = Not for long term holdings. Not as secure as hardware wallet, vulnerable to info stealer malware.

Software/browser wallets are vulnerable because info stealer malware exploits weak security by accessing stored credentials and keys directly on compromised devices.

So while convenient to use, the concept of saving passwords and keys locally becomes a security risk where malware can gain access. This leads to theft of wallet keys, passwords, and ultimately crypto assets without the victim's knowledge until the loss is detected.

And even turning off password saving and autofill reduces the risk. It does not guarantee complete avoidance of sensitive data being stored in memory or caches (like form data), where malware might potentially target it.

Hardware Wallets

Hardware Wallets are the gold standard of self-custody. You can think of them as tiny, ultra secure USB drives.

There are multiple good wallets to chose from. Such as Ledger Nano X, Keystone 3 Pro, Ellipal Titan 2.0, Ngrave Zero and others.

All work in a similar fashion. You connect them to your phone or computer only when transacting with your crypto. Your private keys never leave the device, even when connected and the screen shows you exactly what you are signing. In short, it's almost impossible[15] for malware to steal your keys and access your funds.

- Pros = Bank-level security. Survives phone loss, hacks, and even house fires, floods, etc. As long as your seed phrase is backed up and secure.
- Cons = Slight learning curve (5-10 minutes)
- Best for = longer term holdings and larger amounts of crypto.

Multi-sig Wallets

---

[15] No system is 100% fool proof, so don't believe the "our wallet is 100% malware proof" hype.

Multi-sig or multiple signature wallets are where self-custody requires multiple approvals to send funds, just like requiring two signatures on a check.

The most common set-up is 2 of 3. That is three keys and any two are required to move the funds. So you have one key on your phone, one on your computer and you give one key to a trusted friend, or you keep it in a safe deposit box.

So, even if one key is lost you can still move the funds. Imagine you lose your phone, no problem, one key is not enough. You use the other two to recover. This is how businesses, DAOs, smart individuals and even governments hold their crypto portfolios.

- Pros = Nearly un-hackable. Perfect for long term holds or large amounts of crypto like a couple's savings, etc.
- Cons = Slightly more set-up and slower to access.
- Best for = Anyone who wants bulletproof security and peace of mind.

Your Seed Phrase, Handle with Care.

Your seed phrase is your master-key. Its a random 12 or 24[16] word list like "apple, cat, meadow, etc".

If your device is lost, stolen, or broken, you enter the seed phrase into a new wallet and, snap, your money is back.

---

[16] Some older or customs seed phrases are 18 or 21 words in length

Golden rules for your seed phrase;

- Never store it digitally. No photos, no cloud storage, no emailing it either!
- Write it on paper or use a metal plate designed for seed phrase storage. (Like Billfodl, Cryptosteel, Blockplate, etc). Anyone will work.
- Store in two separate secure locations.
- Never share it with anyone you don't trust.

Common Fears of Self-Custody and Why They are Overblown

1. "I might lose my seed phrase"
Solution = store two copies in separate safe places.

2. "I'm concerned I'll send funds to the wrong address"
Solution = hardware wallets show the address on-screen, just double check it.

3. "Is too complicated"
Solution = setup only takes 15 minutes. You can do it.

4. What if I die and my heirs can't access my crypto"
Solution = share one key with a trusted heir. Multi-sig makes this easy.

The Payoff: Freedom and Savings

When you self-custody:

- No one can freeze your funds

- You avoid exchange fees (1 to 4% per trade)
- You sleep well, knowing where your money is and knowing it is your's

Holding your own keys isn't about distrusting the world. It's about trusting yourself.

It's saying: I am capable. I am responsible. I am in control.

The tools are ready. The risks are known and the path is clear.

Chapter 6 - Earning Yield Like a Whale (But Safely)

Yield farming isn't gambling when your downside is protected and your upside is uncapped. That's just called winning slowly.

John Berry

There are multiple ways to earn in crypto. And that's the difference between a whale and everyone else.

Whales[17] don't hunt yield, they farm it. They don't gamble on 100× tokens, they rent time-tested cash flows from audited protocols. And they never, ever give up custody of their keys.

This chapter is the playbook whales use, rewritten for someone with $10,000 instead of $10 million. The strategies scale down cleanly because they were built for institutions first.

---

17 A whale in cryptocurrency is an individual, institution, or entity that holds a massive amount of a digital asset, often enough to move markets with a single transaction.

Some are more advanced, but DeFi is not rocket science. When I first jumped into DeFi back in the pioneer days (okay it was 2020), I was providing liquidity and yield farming across multiple chains and on numerous protocols. Everything was done manually, no AI to help anyone. And I learnt it all by trying out different dApps, reading blogs and asking questions in Discord groups. Today there are tons of resources, YouTube videos and more to guide you. I don't have the space to create a guide to each DeFi protocol so treat this chapter more as an introductory overview and go deeper from here.

The core insight is simple, real yield in crypto comes from lending scarce capital to people who need it more than you do, on terms that favor the lender. Everything else, meme coins, hot token flips, leveraged plays, is all noise. You can win big, but you can lose equally as much.

The four pillars that follow are the only ones you need if you want to earn yield safely:

- Stablecoin yield farming done the institutional way
- Real-world asset tokenization
- Over-collateralized lending loops
- AI-driven rebalancing

Master these, and you'll earn 5 to 25 percent per year without ever wondering if your exchange will freeze withdrawals.

Stablecoin yield farming

Let start with stablecoins

Stablecoins are the oxygen of DeFi. More than $150 billion worth circulate today, and every dollar of it is someone else's liability.

Circle promises to redeem USDC 1:1.
Tether does the same for USDT.
Likewise Binance and First Digital Labs does the same with FDUSD.

But whales don't hold stablecoins to hoard dollars, they hold them to lend dollars.

The real move is to bridge them to a layer-2 network like Arbitrum, where gas costs pennies, and deposit into a lending protocol that charges borrowers to borrow.

Aave is the largest lending protocol in DeFi. And Aave version 3 is the gold standard. It's been audited more times than most banks, and its governance is controlled by staked AAVE token holders who have skin in the game.

When you deposit USDC into Aave on Arbitrum, you instantly become a liquidity provider. Borrowers, mostly leveraged traders and arbitrage bots, pay variable interest to borrow your capital. That interest accrues to you in real time, visible on the Aave app as a slowly climbing balance.

On a good day in 2025, USDC borrowers pay 6 to 8 percent annualized. On a bad day, it dips to 4 percent. Either way, it beats a savings account.

But whales don't stop at Aave. They earn more yield on Yearn Finance. Yearn is a yield aggregator run by anonymous developers who compete to route capital into the highest-returning vault strategies. Its also one of the original DeFi protocols. And while the USDC vault might keep 60 percent in Aave, 30 percent in Compound, and 10 percent in a Curve liquidity pool, it rebalances every few hours to chase the best rate. The net effect is an extra 1 to 2 percent on top of raw Aave yields, minus a 2 percent management fee and a 20 percent performance cut. After costs, a $10,000 deposit typically returns 7 to 9 % net, compounded weekly. Not bad at all.

Insurance is non-negotiable. Nexus Mutual lets you buy coverage against smart-contract failure. For a Yearn USDC vault, the premium runs 0.5 to 1 percent per year. That's cheap for peace of mind.
If Yearn ever gets hacked, and it hasn't in five years, Nexus pays out in ETH within days.

You can easily convert fiat to USDC on Coinbase or any exchange. Then bridge to Arbitrum via the official portal, deposit into Yearn, and buy Nexus cover, all without ever signing a transaction that sends keys to a third party.

The only custodian is the protocol code itself, and that code has been battle-tested by billions in total value locked.

Real World Asset Strategies

This is where traditional finance meets the blockchain. Real-world assets.

Imagine buying a U.S. Treasury bill that trades on Uniswap, the largest Decentralized exchange. In this case, thats Ondo Finances OUSG Token. Each OUSG represents a share of short-term T-bills held in custody by a regulated broker. The yield comes from the U.S. government, not a DeFi protocol. In 2025, three-month T-bills pay around 5 %. Ondo passes nearly all of it through, minus a 15-basis-point fee. You can enter with $100 and exit the same day. No KYC if you're already on-chain. Then there is the ability to invest in private credit loans, all over-collateralized of course.

Maple Finance is where Institutional borrowers, crypto trading firms, mining operations, real estate funds, all post collateral and borrow USDC for 30 to 90 days. Senior pool lenders earn 8 to 15 %, depending on the borrower's credit rating.

And as mentioned, every loan is over-collateralized by BTC or ETH at 150 % loan-to-value. If the borrower defaults, the collateral is liquidated automatically.

Maple's default rate since inception is under 0.3 %.

Real estate tokenization

Lastly we have real estate tokenization. Platforms like RealT and Centrifuge let you buy fractional ownership in rental properties or commercial mortgages. A $50 token might represent one square foot of a Detroit duplex that pays $0.40 per month in rent.

The cash is deposited into your wallet in USDC on the first of every month. Liquidity varies, some tokens trade on Uniswap, others require a 6-month lock, but the yields range from 7 to 12 percent, all backed by physical collateral.

So what would a balanced portfolio look like?
Half your capital in Ondo T-bills for daily liquidity, 30 percent in Maple's senior pool for higher yield, and 20 percent in a basket of RealT properties for inflation protection.
Blended return of roughly 9.2 %.
Risk profile, lower than a stock index fund.

AI-Rebalancing

This last strategy how whales use to earn yield on assets they never plan to sell, namely Bitcoin.

This is done via depositing 1 BTC worth around $100,000, in a MakerDAO vault and minting DAI stablecoins up to 50 percent loan-to-value. That's $50,000 in cash without triggering a taxable sale.

You swap the DAI for USDC on Curve, slippage is under 1 basis point and deposit the USDC into Aave to earn 6 percent. The interest pays the 2 to 3 % DAI stability fee and leaves you with 3 to 4 % net profit in stablecoins. Your Bitcoin still sits in the vault, accruing in dollar terms if the price rises.

And there is zero liquidation risk at 50 % LTV. Bitcoin would need to drop 50 % in a single day to trigger a penalty, and even then, Maker's emergency shutdown module protects collateral.

If you want more yield, Morpho Blue improves the return by dynamically routing borrowed stablecoins into the highest-yielding lender. Your funds are in Aave one hour, then moved to Compound the next, squeezing out an extra 1 to 2 %.

That's the whale playbook 2026. No leverage. No rugs. Just math, audited code, and the quiet confidence that comes from knowing your capital works harder than you do.

Part IV: Defense & Offense

"The chain is only as strong as its weakest signer. One sloppy click, and the fortress falls in eight seconds."
Anonymous DeFi Auditor, 2024

The night my friend lost 5 Bitcoin still haunts me.
He did everything right but made just one mistake

- He had his seed phrase etched on a Cryptotag, stored in a bank vault
- He ran a Coldcard with dice-rolled entropy, (super secure)
- He never clicked phishing links
- Yet one careless moment, connecting his MacBook to a coffee shop Wi-Fi while signing a transaction let a clipboard hijacker swap the withdrawal address
- Five Bitcoin, gone in eight seconds
- The chain was immutable, no undoing his error
- His coffee became cold
- And the lesson was permanent

Okay time to come clean.

My friend never lost 5 Bitcoin, I wrote this to illustrate how easy it is for smart hackers to steal cryptocurrency if you don't pay attention to your cybersecurity defense.

And this chapter is not about paranoia. It is about proportionate defense. The same rigor a hedge fund or government applies to a billion-dollar treasury applies to your $10,000 portfolio. And especially if your funds live in DeFi, where smart contracts are both your vault and a potential trapdoor.

The fact is attackers don't care about your net worth, they care about your attack surface. That is the total set of vulnerabilities and entry points that an attacker could exploit to compromise your phone of computer.

My goal in this chapter is to shrink that surface to a pinprick using two parallel playbooks, offensive security (active measures that deter and deceive) and defensive security (passive layers that absorb and survive).

We will cover securing your wallet, your network, your computer, and you, the human involved. Plus we will identity DeFi-specific landmines and help you to avoid them.

Sovereignty Defense strategies

Your Wallet

Self-custody is not a product, it is a discipline. (see Chapter 5 for a complete breakdown of how to self-custody securely). Whether you are using a Keystone, Coldcard, Ledger or Trezor wallet, they all ship with secure functionality.

When you set up your wallet, write the seed phrase either on 2 separate sheets of paper and store them apart, in different locations. A safe deposit box is a good option. Or use a metal plate such as Billfodl, Crytotag or Seed plate. Never store the full phrase digitally, even encrypted. A single leaked backup renders every hardware wallet useless.

Passphrases are your second brain. BIP-39 allows a 25th word that acts as a salt. Choose a memorable but non-obvious phrase, something like "sunset harbor 2025", and commit it to muscle memory.

Your Network

Now lets harden your network. Your home IP is a beacon. Route all blockchain traffic through a dedicated VPN endpoint, like ProtonVPN, NordVPN or ExpressVPN. If possible paid in for the VPN with a privacy coin like Monero.

And because DeFi lives on RPC[18] endpoints, never use the default public RPC. Infura, Alchemy, and QuickNode log every request. Switch to a private RPC such as Pocket Network or Ankr Premium.

A private RPC endpoint for DeFi gives you faster, more reliable transactions, avoids rate limits and congestion on

---

[18] An RPC endpoint is a web address where a program can call functions on a remote server.

public nodes, and keeps your trades private to reduce front-running risks.

For layer-2s, use the official bridge endpoints only. Third-party aggregators like Hop or Across can be compromised. When bridging, always verify the contract address on the official docs, not a Discord link. In 2025, fake bridge sites are the #1 DeFi drain vector.

DeFi-specific device rules:

Never sign a DeFi transaction on a machine that has ever run MetaMask with an imported seed. Hot wallets are for viewing, not signing.

And when signing transactions NEVER sign anything that ask for unlimited access to your funds. In 2025, 68 % of DeFi drains come from unlimited ERC-20 approvals. Revoke them weekly via Revoke.cash, using a fresh browser profile each time.

Some additional DeFi best practices to protect you.

- Avoid new protocols with less than $10m TVL. This is where 92% of rug pulls take place. What at least 90 days and see at least two audits before depositing any funds.
- Flash loan governance attacks: Avoid protocols with low quorum (e.g. lease than 100K token votes).
- Avoid bridge hacks. Never use unofficial bridges. Stick to LayerZero, Synapse, or official L2 bridges.
- Never, ever store your seed phrase in any cloud service! Leaks happen more often than you realize.

- Use a desktop/ laptop computer not your mobile. Mobile browsers are malware magnets, you can at least harden a desktop computer.

Chapter 8 - AI Fraud Shield: Catch Hacks Before They Happen

Most people buy the dip after the rug. Smart money buys the AI that prevents it.

DeFi Security Researcher, 2025

Empowering Users to Stay On Step Ahead

It was a routine evening trade for Alex, a freelance developer using DeFi to swap some ETH for stablecoins on Uniswap. The app loaded smoothly, but as the transaction hit the mempool[19], a subtle notification popped up in his MetaMask extension: "*Potential sandwich risk detected, reroute via private relay?*"

Powered by MEV Blocker's AI-driven scanner (https://mevblocker.io/), it had already simulated the frontrunning bots circling his trade, estimating a 2.8% slippage hit. Alex tapped yes. The swap cleared cleanly, with full value intact. No drama, no loss, just a quiet win against the invisible predators of the chain.

---

19 The mempool is a waiting area where unconfirmed blockchain transactions sit before being added to a block.

For individual users like Alex, traders, yield farmers, or anyone else navigating DeFi protocols, this is the new normal in late 2025. You're not a protocol operator with enterprise budgets, you're armed with the personal tools that fit into your wallet or browser, using AI to spot threats before they ruin your day.

No more crossing fingers on every swap. These defenses turn the tables, making fraud and MEV (miner extractable value) attacks as frustrating for hackers as they are rare for you.

Why Individuals Need Their Own Shields in DeFi

DeFi's beauty is its permissionless access.
Anyone with a web3 wallet can lend on Aave, yield farm on Pendle, or arbitrage on 1inch. But this openness invites wolves looking to exploit individual traders

In 2025, individual losses from scams and exploits topped $1.2 billion, per Chainalysis data, with sandwich attacks alone siphoning $150 million from retail traders on DEXs. Phishing sites mimic legit dApps, fake airdrops drain wallet seeds, and MEV bots front-run your trades, turning your profit into their gain.

All the traditional advice, use hardware wallets, double-check URLs, helps, but it's reactive.

AI changes that. It learns your patterns. How you trade, when you connect, what gas you bid. Deviations from the norm scream trouble. For semi-advanced users, this means tools that not only alert but act, simulating outcomes, suggesting tweaks, or auto-routing, all without needing a PhD in blockchain forensics.

The best part? These aren't locked behind paywalls or protocols. They're extensions, mobile apps, and free tiers designed for you, the solo operator. Let's break down the arsenal available today.

Your First Line of Defense: Wallet-Level Guardians

Start where you live: your wallet. MetaMask, the go-to for 80% of DeFi users, rolled out AI-enhanced security in its 2025 updates via partnerships with tools like Sardine and Arkham Intelligence.

Sardine's lightweight AI engine scans incoming connections in real time, flagging suspicious dApps by cross-referencing on-chain behavior with off-chain signals, like a sudden spike in similar wallet drains reported on forums. If a site asks for unlimited approvals, it pauses and explains: *This matches 47 recent phishing vectors, revoke instead?*

And for even deeper protection, you can integrate Trust Wallet's MEV Shield, a browser extension that obfuscates your transaction details before broadcast. Using simple machine learning models trained on mempool data, it predicts bot interference and bundles your trade into

Flashbots' private relay. In tests, it cut sandwich losses by 68% for users swapping over $1,000. Setup is a one-click install; no coding required.

Another company using AI tools to protect users, is Rabby Wallet (https://rabby.io/)

Rabby Wallet takes it further with built-in simulation. Before signing, its AI (powered by Tenderly's backend) forks the chain virtually, replaying your transactions to forecast outcomes. "*This borrow on Compound could trigger liquidation in 3 blocks if ETH dips 2%, adjust collateral?* " It's like having a personal auditor, on your team, catching cases that rules-based checks miss.

DEX and Aggregator Allies: Smart Routing Without the Sting

When you trade, don't go it alone. Lean on aggregators that have added AI defenses.

1inch's Fusion mode is one of them. Upgraded in 2025, uses predictive analytics to route swaps through protected paths, avoiding toxic pools where liquidity providers (often bots) lurk.
Its AI scans for arbitrage opportunities that could sandwich you, then batches your order with others for fair execution.

For a $5,000 USDC-ETH swap, it might shave 1.5% off slippage by timing the mempool just right. The app's dashboard even shows a "risk score" per route, empowering you to choose. 1.5% might not seem much but if you trade often or large amounts, it quickly adds up.

Another is CoW Swap, a favorite for privacy advocates. Its batch auctions, enhanced with AI optimization, match trades off-chain first, then settle on-chain without mempool exposure. The system learns from your history. Prefer low-gas L2s? It prioritizes them, while flagging anomalies like unusual token pairs that signal scams.

In a 2025 case study, users avoided $2.3 million in collective MEV extractions. And its a free to use, with a mobile app for on-the-go checks.

For yield farming, Yearn Finance's vaults now include AI-driven "guardian modes." Before auto-compounding, it simulates flash loan risks, pausing if patterns match historical exploits.

As an individual, you select vaults with this enabled, getting alerts via Telegram: "*High recon activity detected hold off on deposit.*"

I've personally used Yearn Finance for several years and really like the platform.

Challenges and Smarts: Using Them Wisely

No anti-fraud shield is perfect. False alerts can annoy during volatile markets, and privacy-focused users might balk at data-sharing (opt for ZK-enabled ones like those in Veritas Protocol's user toolkit).

Start small. Install one extension, test on small trades. Combine them, MetaMask + 1inch, for layered defense.

Cost? Mostly free or under $10/month for basics.

Time investment? Five minutes to onboard, then passive protection.

Its worth it!

The Horizon: 2026 and Beyond for Everyday Users

By 2026/27, expect AI companions in every wallet. Think Grok-like agents in MetaMask that whisper, "*This yield farm's APY is inflated by a governance attack; pivot to this safer one?* "

Simulations will run locally on your device via zkML, keeping data private while predicting exploits with 95% accuracy.

In 2027, "personal immune systems" emerge. AI that auto-revokes approvals on dormant wallets, negotiates better rates via intent-based solvers, and even sues scammers on-chain with tokenized evidence.

Forecasts from Gartner forecast 75% of DeFi users adopting these by then, slashing individual losses by 80%.

Tools like zkAGI prototypes hint at on-device training, where your transaction history anonymously bolsters global models.

Expect attackers to push back with AI-generated deepfakes and polymorphic phishing, but user tools will counter with biometric proofs, fingerprint-linked approvals, and cross-wallet federations sharing threat intel without doxxing.

The battle will never end, but AI can really give smart users who are willing to take the time, the advantage.

Sovereignty Fix: Your AI Fraud Shield Strategy

In 2025's DeFi, the empowered user isn't the one with the biggest bag, it's the one with the smartest shields.

Start today.

Try the tools mentioned throughout this chapter. Lean into the ones you like and make them part of your everyday routine.

And continue to adapt. New tool innovation never stops. I've tried to listed some of the best I'm aware of, but this is not an exhaustive list.

Chapter 9 - Regulatory Moats & Exit Ramps

The DeFi jungle is full of 100 × gems and zero exits. The fortress has 8% plus and a door that stays open when the music stops.

Imagine this: You've spent the last two years building a solid sovereign wallet.

Your Bitcoin is self-custodied, your AI agent is quietly compounding yields in DeFi, and tokenized U.S. Treasuries are paying you 4–6% with almost no effort. Life feels good, until you need to pay taxes, buy a house, or simply want to spend some of those gains on a vacation.

Suddenly, the "decentralized" dream hits the very centralized reality of governments, banks, and tax authorities. This can be a wake up call for many.[20]

This chapter is about the bridges between your on-chain world and the off-chain one.

We'll call the protective rules that keep bad actors out regulatory moats, and the safe ways to turn crypto back into spendable money exit ramps.

---

[20] I'm not an attorney or a tax or financial advisor of any sort. Please don't take anything in this chapter as legal, tax or financial advice. See disclaimer in front of book for more details.

Its important you understand the both if you want sleep well knowing your wealth is both free and protected.

The World in Late 2025: Two Different Playgrounds

As I write this in November 2025, the regulatory map looks wildly different depending on where you live.

In the United States the second Trump administration has taken the opposite path to previous administrations. After years of confusion and enforcement actions, 2025 finally brought much needed real clarity and enthusiasm to the broader cryptocurrency and blockchain industries.

The GENIUS Act has created a proper federal framework for stablecoins and digital assets. The SEC and CFTC finally have clear lanes to operate and Bitcoin ETFs are everywhere (with trillions in inflows).
The new administration openly talks about America becoming the "crypto capital of the world."

Companies that fled the U.S. in 2022–2024 are rushing back.

Across the Atlantic, in Europe, the Markets in Crypto-Assets regulation (MiCA) is fully live. If an exchange or stablecoin issuer wants to serve Europeans, they need a license, proper reserves, and strict anti-money-laundering rules.

This has made Europe feel "safe" for mainstream money. Big banks are launching tokenized funds and stablecoins, but it's also expensive and slow for startups.

The effect has been that many innovative DeFi teams have simply decided not to serve EU citizens rather than jump through the hoops.

What does this mean for you? Simple geography can make your life easier or harder.

A U.S. resident today has more licensed on-ramps, better Bitcoin, Ether and Solana ETFs, and clearer rules for tokenized real-world assets (RWAs) like treasury funds from BlackRock or Franklin Templeton and others.

Europeans may enjoy some strong consumer protection but fewer cutting-edge options.

Sovereignty Fix: Leveraging Moats

The smart sovereign individual often uses both worlds. Hold the risky high-yield stuff in privacy-friendly chains, but park stable wealth in regulated, tokenized products that enjoy these new moats.

Why Regulatory Moats Are Your Friend

A "moat" in business is something that protects a good company from competition. In crypto, real regulation is starting to act like a moat, for the good guys that is.

Think about stablecoins.

For years we worried that Tether (USDT) might not have full reserves. Today, under clearer U.S. rules and MiCA in Europe, new-generation stablecoins like USDC, EURC, and regulated yield-bearing ones must prove 1:1 backing, get audited regularly, and allow instant redemption.

That's a moat that works for you and me. Scammy issuers get shut out, and your money is safer.

The same is happening with tokenized real-world assets. BlackRock's BUIDL fund, the largest tokenized U.S. Treasury fund by a wide margin, crossed $3 billion in 2025. (At the time of writing its a little less). In the years ahead though its bound to grow as demand of tokenized RWA's continues its explosive growth.

Ondo Finance, Franklin Templeton, and others let you own fractions of bonds, money-market funds, and even private credit, all directly on-chain, 24/7, with real legal backing.

And these aren't wild DeFi experiments! They're regulated products from century-old institutions.

The regulation is the moat that lets your grandma's pension fund buy in without freaking out.

For you, this means higher yields with lower risk. Instead of lending USDC on a random protocol for 8% (and praying the team doesn't rug[21]), you can earn 4 to 6% on tokenized Treasuries or AAA-rated credit.

And unlike the early wild-west days of DeFi, it's all legally enforceable off-chain if something goes wrong.

Exit Ramps: Turning Crypto Back into Real Life

Probably the hardest part of financial freedom isn't making money. It's spending it without destroying your gains or privacy.

As a DeFi user with self-custodied assets (e.g., in MetaMask, Ledger, or Phantom), your priority is bridging from on-chain stablecoins (USDC, USDT, ETH) to fiat (USD, EUR, etc.) with minimal custody control, low fees, and tax compliance.

Spending or selling crypto is almost always a taxable event in the US/EU/UK (capital gains on profits, income on yields), so the "legal" way is simply to report it properly using tools like Koinly or CoinTracker.

There are no magic zero-tax loopholes for most residents.

Here are the best, most practical exit ramps available right now in late 2025:

---

21 Take the money and disappear

- Wallet-embedded sell-to-bank off ramps (Ramp Network, Transak, MoonPay, etc). Services like MoonPay, Ramp Network, and Mercuryo are now embedded in most non-custodial wallets (MetaMask, Phantom, etc.). You connect to your bank, sell USDC/EURC, and the money lands in your account in minutes. Fees have dropped to 0.5–1.5% in most countries. All direct bank transfers from your wallet should provide a 1099 (US) and easy CSV export for taxes. Perfect for everyday cash-outs.

- Crypto debit cards. The perfect app for everyday spending. Coinbase Card, Crypto.com Visa, and new entrants like Fold or Strike let you spend USDC or Bitcoin directly, converting at the point of sale with almost no fees. Most offer a cashback, often 1 to 4% in Bitcoin. In Europe, cards from licensed providers work the same way under MiCA regulations.

- Tokenized RWA Redemption. Sell the tokens on-chain and off-ramp the stablecoins instantly. These funds typically tokenize underlying assets like U.S. Treasuries, money market instruments, or private infrastructure, and they are increasingly accessible to retail users through platforms with low minimums, KYC processes, and compliance features. Tokens are burned via smart contracts, triggering a fiat payout to a linked bank account. Processing is 1to 3 business days, with some offering intraday options. Yields are distributed automatically in USD or stablecoins.

- Regulated Exchanges with Direct Bank Links Coinbase, Kraken, Gemini (U.S.), and licensed European platforms like Bitstamp or Kraken let you sell crypto and withdraw straight to your bank account in 1 to 3 days, often for free or under 1%. If you're in the U.S., these are fully KYC'd but feel like using a normal brokerage.

The US Tax Reality Check

Sorry, there's no escaping this one.

- Selling or swapping crypto (even to stablecoins) = capital gains tax.
- DeFi yields, staking rewards, liquidity mining = ordinary income the moment you receive them.
- Hold longer than one year → long-term capital gains (0–20%, much friendlier).

In 2025 the IRS finally gets Form 1099-DA from every major exchange and many DeFi front-ends. They know what you did.

The good news? Tools like Koinly, (my personal favorite), ZenLedger, and CoinTracker make reporting almost automatic.

Pro tip: Harvest losses every year (sell losers to offset winners), or consider moving to Puerto Rico (Act 60) or a crypto-friendly country if you're sitting on life-changing gains.

(Talk to a real tax advisor—this isn't advice!)

Sovereignty Fix: Building Your Personal Moat + Ramp Strategy

Here's the simple playbook most sovereign wallets use today:

- Core wealth → Self-custodied Bitcoin + regulated tokenized Treasuries/RWAs (moat-protected yield).
- Spending money → USDC/EURC in a wallet with a debit card or built-in off-ramp.
- High-yield experiments → Smaller allocation to pure DeFi, accepting the risk.
- Annual clean-up → Sell enough to cover taxes/living expenses through regulated ramps, harvest losses, repeat.

Final thoughts re Moats & Ramps

The era of pure Wild West crypto is ending. And that's actually good news. Real regulatory moats are keeping the scammers out and letting institutions pour billions in. Smart exit ramps mean you can finally enjoy your gains without jumping through ridiculous hoops.

Financial freedom isn't about escaping the system entirely, it's about using the best parts of both worlds.

Build your sovereign life inside the strongest moats, and know which exit ramps to use, when.

When the next bull run comes, and it will, you'll be ready not just to ride it, but to step off whenever you choose, richer and freer than ever.

Part V: The Sovereign Life

Chapter 10 - AI-Powered Financial Coaching in Your Pocket

"For the first time in history, the world's best financial advisor charges nothing, fits in your pocket, never sleeps, never takes a vacation, and already knows your cost basis better than your CPA."

John Berry

It was 2:17 a.m. in Austin. I'd just come off a brutal twelve-hour trading session, nursing a mild headache and staring at a fresh $10,000 USDC transfer sitting in my wallet. I was trying to decide whether to park it in a low-risk tokenized Treasury fund or let it ride on a leverage position I'd been eyeing.

My phone buzzed with a single calm notification:
"Aria. If you put the full $10,000 into USDY right now, you'll lock in 4.35% annualized with daily payouts and zero duration risk. The alternative loop you're looking at (USDC → ETH → perp long) has a 68% chance of wiping the principal in the next 72 hours at current volatility. Want me to show you the breakeven chart, or just send it to Ondo?"

I hadn't typed a word. The wallet had watched my open tabs, noticed the pending transfer from Coinbase, pulled the latest Treasury rates, and stress-tested the leverage idea I'd been circling for two days.
I exhaled, half-annoyed, half-relieved.

"Fine," I muttered. "Do the boring thing."
One tap later, the $10,000 was swapped into USDY, tokens minted, and the first day's yield already accruing.

That was the moment I realized my pocket now carried a coach that was smarter, faster, and crucially cheaper than any Discord alpha group, paid signal service, or even my own sleep-deprived brain at 2 a.m.

For the first time in years of trading crypto, I wasn't alone with my greed and my FOMO.

I had Aria.

So how Close Are We to a Service Like Aria?

The short answer. We're already here, prototypes and early products are live today, as of November 2025, delivering 70-80% of Aria's vision in non-custodial wallets.

If Aria represents a pocket-sized AI coach that reads your on-chain activity, simulates risks, forecasts outcomes, and nudges you toward optimal moves (like parking $10K in Ondo over a risky perp trade) *without* touching your keys, then the gap is shrinking fast. We're talking perhaps 6 to12 months for mainstream polish and broader adoption, driven by agentic AI on blockchains like Warden Protocol and integrations in apps like Binance Wallet.

The whole tech stack, from on-device LLMs, ZK proofs for privacy, and DeFi oracles, is mature enough that "shipping" is the bottleneck, not invention.

For context, Aria's core features (from the story, wallet monitoring, yield/risk simulation, natural-language nudges) align with what's emerging in "AI agents" for crypto.

These aren't gimmicks, they're autonomous systems that query your holdings via read-only access, pull real-time data (e.g., Treasury yields from Chainlink), and output prescriptive advice.

The revolution isn't hypothetical.

It's in beta testing, with millions of daily interactions already.

Note while many of the capabilities I've outlined in this chapter are "future tech". However they are all real and will be available soon, depending on when you read this.

From Static Wallet to Dynamic Coach

Traditional self-custodial wallets are really glorified keychains. They hold assets, they are used to sign transactions and maybe stake. The new sovereign wallets we will all soon be using will be more of a real-time control tower running three parallel brains:

- A deterministic blockchain brain (with your keys, running your rules)

- A privacy-preserving data brain (on-device machine learning model + zero-knowledge attestations)

- A large reasoning model brain (fine-tuned on capital-markets data, tax code, and behavioral finance, etc)

These "three brains" will all talk to each other without ever exposing your private keys or your full financial graph to a third party. The result will be a financial coach that can move from reactive. So instead of "You just received 18,400 USDC from Coinbase" you will get a predictive "Park the $18,400 into Ondo before 23:59 UTC tonight. The yield window resets in 4 hours and locks you out of 4.12% for 30 days, it's 312 bps over holding raw USDC and keeps you fully liquid for the next long you're stalking, with zero gap risk".

It's not a generic wealth-manager bot telling you giving generic advice.

It's an intelligent, pro-active trading smart-assistant / coach that speaks in liquidations, basis points, and UTC deadlines, and never lets you waste opportunities because you were too tired or too jaded to run the numbers yourself.

The Four Things Only an AI Coach Can Do 24/7

For retail traders, here are the capabilities that no human advisor, however expensive, will be able to match at scale, and no $99/ month Telegram trading channel will be able to offer at midnight, when the market is bleeding or pumping.

- Sub-second liquidation forecasting with your exact margin stack
  Before you even hit "confirm" on that 25× SOL perp, your AI coach has already simulated the next 4-hour volatility cone using live Pyth/Chainlink feeds, factored in your exact funding rate, cross-exchange collateral (yes, it will see your Bybit, Hyperliquid, and dYdX margin in one view), and tells you:
  "Price needs to drop another 9.4% to liquidate you. That's a 1-in-6.8 event in the next 12 hours. Still want 25× or should we dial it to 11× and survive a 22% wick?"

No human is running that math in real time. Ever!

- Instant, chain-aware tax-lot picker that actually saves you money. You've got BTC, with different cost basis sitting in three different wallets. Here is how you can give yourself a big tax bill with one click. You wanted to move 0.4 BTC into Aave (wrapping first at WBTC and borrow USDC) to invest) so you can earn a safe 4% while waiting for the next bull leg. Nothing fancy, just being responsible for once.So you a wallet, see the 0.4 BTC sitting there, and hit "send." Simple. What you didn't realize was that the wallet was about to pick the coins you bought in 2022 at $18,000 each. Those cheap, dusty coins would have turned a "safe parking move" into a massive taxable event.You was literally one tap away from turning free yield into a tax disaster. Then your phone buzzes. Aria (the AI coach in your wallet has stopped the transaction and said. *"Hey, don't use those 2022 coins yet. That'll cost you $28k in tax for no reason. I'm grabbing the 0.4 BTC from the batch you bought last month instead, the tax is basically zero and you still get the full 4%. Okay?"* You stared at the screen, gulp when you realize your mistake, and tapped "yes", thankful you installed Aria! One path cost you almost nothing, the other would have wrecked your whole year.

- Live MEV-protected routing + flash-loan-aware execution
  Your AI coach doesn't just send your swap to Uniswap and pray. It routes it through CowSwap, 1inch Fusion, or PRCL based on current MEV conditions, automatically bundles with Flashbots Protect or SUAVE, and tells you.
  "Direct route = 41 bps slippage + sandwich risk. Bundled private route = 6 bps slippage and $187 saved. Executing in 11 seconds on the next block."
  That's free money on every rotation.

- Cross-protocol yield scanner that never misses a window
  Every hour your AI financial coach will scan Ondo, Morpho Blue, Pendle, Maple, Figure, and twenty smaller venues for the highest risk-adjusted USDC/USDT yield. When a 48-hour 28% APY arbitrage window opens on Morpho because some whale just created a new vault, it pings you.
  "New vault live! 28.4% APY for the next 41 hours only. $9,200 move gets you $178 extra vs. current BUIDL spot. Zero IL, same-day exit. One-tap deploy?"

These four aren't coming in 2027. They're pretty much live right now inside wallets like Armor, Warden, and the new Binance AI layer.

The only difference between the traders who stay don't make it and the ones who quietly compound at 18 to 20 % and more net is whether they've turned to an AI financial coach yet.

The Architecture That Makes It Possible (Without Sacrificing Sovereignty)

Privacy guaranteed tech includes:

On-device inference
- Apple Neural Engine/ Qualcomm Hexagon
- Your keys and raw data never leave the secure enclave, no external AI has access.

Selective disclosure
- ZK- attestations and Nocturne-style accounts (two privacy-preserving techs that let you prove financial facts)
- Prove income or net worth without revealing addresses

Off-chain data oracle
- Chainlink + Pyth + custom LLM scrapers
- Signed data feeds

Reasoning engine
- Fine-tuned Llama-3.2-70B or Mixtral-8x22B
- Runs locally or via threshold-encrypted MPC cloud (cloud-based platforms and services that leverage Multi-Party Computation (MPC), a cryptographic technique for secure, collaborative computing to enable privacy-preserving operations at scale.

User interface
- Natural language and adaptive visualizations
- Will feel like iMessage with a CFA (Chartered Financial Analyst) in your pocket

The magic is that the most sensitive computations like private key operations and tax-lot selection will all happen entirely on-device.

The large reasoning model only ever sees encrypted gradients or ZK proofs. You remain in full control, yet you receive advice that previously required a many thousand dollar per month retainer.

Personally I can't wait to fully implement this for myself!

The Regulatory Landscape (As of Q4 2025)

- United States. The SEC has explicitly stated that non-custodial wallets providing "investment advice" via AI may trigger the Investment Advisers Act if they exercise discretion. The winning architecture therefore requires the human to be in the loop for final execution (one-tap approval, not fully automated).
- Singapore & Hong Kong. MAS and SFC have both green-lit "restricted digital advisory" models where the AI can give personalized advice if the underlying wallet remains non-custodial.
- EU. MiCA Article 78 carves out self-custodial tools from the full advisory regime, giving Europe an unexpected lead in sovereign AI deployment.

The Next 18 Months: What Ships Next

- Voice-first coaching (you'll talk to your wallet the way you talk to Siri, but with CFA-level answers)

- Cross-chain collateral optimization (you will be able to borrow against your Solana staked positions to buy Franklin Templeton's BENJI at the best rate)
- Embedded legal-entity creation (set up a Wyoming DAO or a Cayman foundation with one prompt, pre-funded with tokenized Treasuries)
- Predictive estate planning (the coach will tell you the exact date your estate tax hits zero under current law and suggest moves today that save your heirs eight figures)
- On-device 70B-parameter models capable of reading entire tax codes in context. This is a near-future capability where massive large language models (LLMs), with 70 billion parameters that will run entirely on your smartphone or laptop. These models will be able to ingest and reason over huge documents, like the full U.S. Internal Revenue Code (all 4 million words).

Sovereignty Fix to the end of "Trust Me"

For decades, wealth management was built on asymmetric information. The advisor knew more than the client, so the client paid for access to that knowledge.

The sovereign wallet with an AI coach reverses the asymmetry. The client now knows, in real time, exactly what every basis point costs, exactly what every tax election saves, exactly what every borrowing option yields.

The relationship is no longer "trust me."
It is "verify me."

And when verification becomes instantaneous, continuous, and free, the old fee structures will collapse under their own weight.

Welcome to the age of financial sovereignty.

The revolution will not be centralized.

Chapter 11 - The Family Office of One

*"A man with a watch knows what time it is.
A man with two watches is never sure.
A man with a family office of one knows exactly what time it is, because he built the watch himself."*

Naval Ravikant (Wealth philosopher), 2025 (tweeted March 14, 2025, 11:47 UTC)

*"The family office is dead.
Long live the family office of one."*

Erik Voorhees (@ErikVoorhees), October 2025

How to Run a Billion-Dollar Playbook with a $50,000 Portfolio

You don't need a surname on a Forbes list to run like a family office.

You just need the same tools they quietly adopted in 2024–2025, shrunk down to fit in your pocket and paid for in satoshis instead of seven-figure retainers.

Welcome to the Family Office of One. A single human, armed with self-custody, tokenized real-world assets, and an always-on AI staff, running a tighter, smarter, more tax-efficient operation than 95% of the multi-family offices that still mail out 180-page glossy reports twice a year.

This is not a fantasy for 2027.

This is shipping today, and the people quietly compounding at 18 to 20% and more, net while working 20 hours a month already live it.

Part I: What a Real Family Office Actually Does (and Why You Can Do It Better)

First lets define what an actual real family office actually does.

Traditional family offices have five core functions:

1. Asset allocation & manager selection

2. Tax planning & estate structuring
3. Risk management & insurance
4. Concierge bill-pay, lifestyle, and philanthropy
5. Reporting, compliance, and governance

Plus add in about a dozen humans and $1 to $3 million in fees, p.a. (Most family offices charge annual fees that typically range between 0.75% and 2% of the family's assets under management (AUM).

So what could your family office of one looks like?

Traditional Family Office	Family Office of One	Cost to You
Chief Investment Officer	On-device AI + Chainlink oracles	$0
Tax Partner	On device cost basis engine + tax LLM	$0
Risk & Insurance team	Real time value at risk & scenario modeling in your wallet	$0

CFO	AI agnets that pay the rent, taxes and invoices in USDC	Approx. $50 p.m.
Quarterly 100 page reports	Live dashboard with a summary every morning	$0

Tool like this are not fiction or 2027 ready either, they are here right now.

- Kyber Network powers decentralized liquidity hubs integrated into various crypto wallets (like Ledger and MyEtherWallet), allowing seamless in-app token swaps, multi-chain trading at optimal rates, and portfolio rebalancing without intermediaries, making it ideal for DeFi users seeking efficient asset management.

- Griffin Wallet, a Solana-native DeFAI wallet with multi-agent AI swarms that handle on-device LLM-driven yield optimization and automated rebalancing. Its cost basis engine tracks historical transaction data on-chain for real-time gain/loss reporting, integrating with tools like Pendle for structured products. Users input natural language intents (e.g., "Optimize my USDC with low risk"), and the on-device model simulates scenarios before execution, reducing cloud dependency for privacy.

- Edwin Terminal Wallet, is a chatbot-integrated wallet blending LLMs (e.g., Claude or LangChain variants) for on-device intent processing across Solana, Base, and

EVM chains. It features a built-in cost basis module that simulates trade impacts on your portfolio's unrealized gains before signing, supporting protocols like Uniswap and Jupiter. Ideal for beginners, it executes swaps or liquidity provision via voice/text commands while keeping computations device-side for sovereignty.

- Infinite Labs Wallet, is an agentic wallet uses on-device AI for goal-based strategies (e.g., "Maximize yield under 5% drawdown"), with a robust cost basis engine that fine-tunes models on your transaction history for personalized tax simulations. LLMs run locally via distributed compute, enabling non-custodial execution on Base and Ethereum L2s—perfect for users prioritizing privacy in volatile markets.

These are just a few of the tools available right now, with many more in testing. The future of AI empowered crypto wallets that trade, rebalance and provide smarter answers than most humans is here right now and will only accelerate in the future.

A Day in the Life of an AI-Crypto Trader

So how does this all play out in practice? Lets look at Sally, a remote crypto trader.

Sally wakes up in Miami and grabs a coffee. Her phone vibrates.

"Morning brief.

- *Net worth +$1629 overnight (yield + SOL long position)*
- *Current run rate yield: 14.5% USD equivalent*
- *Tax-lot harvested $10600 in losses yesterday -> will offset Q4 estimated payment.*
- *Rent auto-paid in USDC 5 hours ago.*
- *New Centrifuge pool opened at 19.2% - deploying $50k in 11 minutes unless you say no?*

Sally sips her coffee, thumbs "approve" and goes to meet a friend for breakfast.

That briefing and single "thumb-approve" use executed the same workflow that would have in a traditional family office required:

- A call to the Chief Investment officer
- A tax director modeling the tax loss
- Writing a rent check
- A credit analyst approving the new pool
- A compliance officer signing off

Time and cost for the old way, approximately 4 to 12 hours and around $2000 in fees.

Sally's new way, 10 seconds and $0 fees.

This is why tech savvy investors and traders are rapidly adopting AI powered crypto wallets right now.

The Tax Game You Finally Win

So one area where traditional family offices with their army of tax planners are always busy is saving their wealthy clients taxes.

Traditional family offices spend millions moving between states, setting up GRATs, and borrowing against art.

You can win with 3 simple moves.

1. Your loss-harvesting bot runs quarterly selling losers and buying buys the identical tokens again 31 days later. This is a fully automated tax-loss harvesting loop. Every quarter (or opportunistically), it scans your wallet for any position showing an unrealized loss. It sells the losing position, instantly realizing a capital loss on-chain.
This loss can now offset capital gains elsewhere in your portfolio (crypto gains, stock gains, etc.). Up to $3,000/year of excess losses can also offset ordinary income.
Next to keep you fully invested the entire time (no market timing risk), the bot immediately buys an equivalent or a highly correlated tokenized asset.
Exactly 31 days later, the bot sells the replacement token position and buys back your original asset.
The 30-day wash-sale window is over and you now have the same economic exposure you started with, but you have

permanently booked a realized capital loss that reduces your taxes this year.

2. Borrow instead of sell. Use IBCOs[22] or Aave collateralized loans at 2 to 4% against your BTC. Never trigger a taxable event.

3. This one is bit more extreme for many, but if you are flexible in where you live and want to save taxes, Relocate to Puerto Rico, Dubai, Portugal NHR, or El Salvador. Tax rates run from 0% for ex-pats, upwards.

Fix: The Technology Stack Required

You do not need permission, a license, or a trust officer in the Caymans. The six things you do need:

- A proper sovereign wallet like an Armor, Warden, Keystone + dynamic multi-sig + passkeys. One master seed, multiple spending policies (daily limits, whitelist-only, 2-of-3 recovery).

- Tokenized cash & treasuries
  Ondo OUSG, RY T-Bill funds, or RWUSD on Binance. This is your new "cash sweep" earning 4.1–4.8% with same-day exits.

---

22 Interest-Bearing Collateral Option, a structured product or protocol feature that allows BTC holders to deposit their Bitcoin as collateral for loans while earning yield on that collateral itself

Note: All there DeFi platforms, OUSG, RY T-bills, and RWUSD, offer tokenized access to U.S. Treasury bills or similar low-risk assets, blending traditional finance yields (around 4-5% APY) with blockchain efficiency.

OGSG from Ondo has limited to accredited/qualified investors globally, with $100K minimum via onboarding/KYC. Retail investors can however gain exposure indirectly through DeFi lending on Flux Finance without accreditation.

RY T-Bills is fully open to any individual with a compatible wallet and no accreditation needed. Users deposit directly into vaults for automated T-bill-linked yields.

RWUSD is open to all Binance users and no accreditation or minimum beyond stablecoin deposit. Its non-transferable but is an easy on-ramp for retail investors.

- Private credit Investments. Put 10–25% in Centrifuge tins[23], Maple pools, or Hamilton Lane's tokenized infra fund. Yields run from 8 to 18% USD, with quarterly liquidity and KYC once.

- AI agents running 24/7

---

23 The term originates from "Tinlake," Centrifuge's Ethereum-based marketplace launched in 2020, and TIN is a core ERC-20 token for these pools.

Agent #1: Yield Maximizer that scans 40+ venues[24] every hour, rebalances automatically via Gelato or Chainlink Automation.

Agent #2: A Tax Guardian that tracks every lot, harvest losses quarterly and flags wash-sale traps before you click.

Agent #3: A Cash-flow Pilot that pays your mortgage, taxes, and credit card the moment stablecoin yield posts, so you're never late and never hold idle fiat.

- A legal wrapper (optional but smart)
  A Wyoming DAO LLC or Cook Islands trust that owns the wallet address. Costs $2 to 5k one-time setup cost, zero ongoing fees and bullet-protects everything from lawsuits and divorce courts.

- Your reporting layer
  Nansen + DeBank + Zerion + custom wallet dashboard → one-screen view of your net worth, yield accrual, tax exposure, and concentration risk. Takes 30 seconds to glance every morning.

The total monthly cost for the entire Sovereign technology stack should be under $120.

---

24 "Venues" is DeFi jargon for the diverse liquidity and yield-generating platforms where assets can be deployed.These aren't physical places but digital protocols, DEXs (decentralized exchanges), or lending markets that act as "hosts" for yield farming.

Sure beats the traditional family office costs!

Final Comments

The ultra-rich didn't build their wealth by handing over 1–2% a year to someone else. They built it by controlling their keys, their cost basis, their borrowing, and their tax exposure.

Everything they once paid millions for, GRATs, loss-harvesting loops, yield-bearing collateral, offshore residency, private-credit access, is now live on-chain and available to anyone with a wallet and the decision to act.

This isn't about joining a family office, it's about becoming your own.

Your tools are already available to go into your pocket:

- On-device agents that optimize yield and harvest losses 24/7
- Permissionless loans against BTC that pay you while you borrow
- Tokenized funds and structures that used to require a $10M minimum and are now open to anyone

All that's missing is your signature on the transaction.

The Family Office of One isn't coming, it's already here.

Unlock it.

Chapter 12 - Forward to the future.

"By 2030 the only people still paying 35 to 55 % of their gains to tax authorities and 1to 2 % a year to middlemen will be the ones who chose nostalgia over sovereignty.

The rest of us simply woke up, pressed 'allow,' and never looked back."

Paul, 36, net worth $4.1 million, effective tax rate 0 %, staff size, one phone.

A day in the life of Paul …

06.45.

Paul wakes up.
His phone, clipped to the nightstand in biometric mode pulses soft sky blue.

"Morning brief" he says.

Aira's calm voice answers through bone-conduction.

"Net worth delta overnight, +$4,720. 58% BTC, 42% automated yield.

Your quarterly loss-harvesting swarm realized $74,000 in offsets yesterday, enough to wipe your entire 2029 tax bill."

"Your Dubai e-residency renewal auto-paid at 03:11 and your El Salvador 90-day presence waiver was filed and accepted. Coffee?"

The machine downstairs is already humming.

Paul is 36, a former quant developer, now happily "unemployed."

He hasn't touched a centralized exchange UI in four years. Everything runs from his sovereign wallet and a swarm of on-device agents.

07.45 - walking to the tram.

Aria again.

"Paul, three decisions need your voice today.

Firstly, the Hamilton Lane 2030 private-credit token (HL-CR30) first-loss tranche is at 19.4% IRR, your agent pre-qualified you for $240,000.

Secondly, the new Babylon Phase-4 staking window just opened. Locking 18 months of BTC collateral drops your effective borrow rate from 1.2% to 1.1%. You'd be paid to stay leveraged.

And last, GRAT-6 matures in 41 days. The successor agent recommends rolling into the new BUIDL-v2 perpetuals at 5.7% that still qualify for Portugal's 0% foreign-income rule."

Paul thinks for a moment, all three options are good and he gives approval for all three to proceed.

Time taken, under a minute. Total gas fees across five different chains, under a $1.

14.30 - the macro view

Paul asks Aira to show him "his macro view" .

The living room wall lights up with one unified balance sheet.

Paul asks *"What if the Fed cuts 200 bps emergency next week?"*

Aira runs 50,000 "paths[25]" in under 2 seconds.

"97th-percentile drawdown = 6.8%.
Tax-optimized plan ready. Harvest $920k embedded losses, rotate short-term T-bills to 2030 munis, bump BTC collateral buffer 9%. Execute on trigger?"

He gives approval. The plan arms itself. Ready to execute should the Fed cut 200 bps.

---

25 A path = one complete simulated future of the entire world (or at least of everything that affects Paul's portfolio). Each single path contains thousands of individual calculations.

22.07 - If I do nothing …

Paul stands on his balcony feeling the Atlantic breeze.

He asks Aira *"If I do absolutely nothing new for ten years, where are we?"*

Aire projects one number in the air.

In 10 years time your $4.1M will turn into $51to 68M (real, after-tax, 95th-percentile path). "That's just the current agents running on autopilot," she adds.

Paul grins, raises his glass, and says the line that has become the new "good night" for an entire generation:

"Keep the keys cold. Wake me if something actually matters."

His wallet pulses once in acknowledgment and dims.

AI agents never sleep and it no longer requires hundreds of millions to run them.

The Five Big Shifts That Made This Possible (2025 → 2030)

1. Sovereign Wallets Became the New Bank Account

By 2027 the smartphone manufacturers shipped the Secure Enclave v4 with 45 GB of isolated NPU memory and hardware zero-knowledge accelerators. That single hardware upgrade turned every phone into a fortress capable of running full 70B-parameter models locally and signing 50+ cross-chain transactions per second. Seed phrases died. Biometric intent + ZK-proof-of-personhood became the standard. Your phone literally became your family office.

2. Agentic AI Went From Chatbot to Chief Financial Officer

Today's on-device models are hybrids. 8B "fast" model for conversation, 70–120B "reasoning" model for planning, and hundreds of fine-tuned micro-agents (tax-loss, borrow-optimizer, residency-tracker, K-1 parser, GRAT manager). They speak every major blockchain natively and negotiate directly with one another in encrypted swarm sessions. Trust is enforced through verifiable computation and reputation oracles. You no longer manage money, you manage agents.

3. Tax Residency Became a Subscription

Portugal's NHR ended in 2024, but five new jurisdictions (Paraguay, Panama, Ras Al Khaimah, Malta 2.0, and a revitalized Greece) launched competing "Digital Nomad Sovereign" programs. Physical presence requirements dropped to 30–90 days per year, and wallets now auto-track location via privacy-preserving geoproofs. Switch primary tax residency with one signed transaction and a $15K–$45K annual fee. The ultra-rich used to spend millions moving between states; now individuals do it for the cost of a nice vacation.

4. Credit Moved On-Chain and Never Left

Private credit, trade finance, aircraft leases, and music royalties are all tokenized and fractional. The average accredited-but-not-institutional investor now holds 15–25% of net worth in senior secured on-chain credit yielding 9–16%, with same-day liquidity and no K-1 if you route through a Cayman or BVI tokenized feeder. The 60/40 portfolio is dead. The new baseline is 40% BTC, 30% on-chain private credit, 20% tokenized T-bills, 10% alpha-capture agents.

5. Regulation Caught Up – But in the Right Way

The turning point was the 2028 U.S. "Personal Financial Agent Act" which created a safe-harbor for on-device agents that use only verifiable compute and disclose all logic in plain language. Europe followed with the AI-Wallet Directive. Suddenly, running your own automated GRAT, cross-border yield optimizer, or perpetual loss-harvester became explicitly legal and protected.

2030, Industries and Professions That No Longer Exist in Recognizable Form

- Traditional retail brokerage (99% market share gone to self-directed agentic wallets)
- Most CPAs doing high-net-worth planning (replaced by specialized tax-agents + human oversight only for $100M+ clients)
- Offshore incorporation middlemen (everything is one-click via wallet-integrated DAOs)

- Paper-based family offices under $250M AUM (economically unviable)
- Manual DeFi yield farming (now fully autonomous)

Professions That Exploded

- Agent auditors (human + AI teams that certify agent logic for ultra-high-net-worth families)
- Jurisdiction arbitragers (designing new 0–4% tax residencies)
- On-chain credit originators (replacing regional banks)
- ZK-identity architects (proof-of-personhood without revealing identity)
- Reputation oracle operators

What the Technology Stack Looks Like in 2030

- Identity. Humanity Protocol + Worldcoin v3 + national eIDs linked via zk bridges
- Wallet OS. fork of iOS/Android with full isolated rollup per app (your Hamilton Lane position lives in its own chain, your BTC in another, unified UI)
- Execution. Intent-centric solvers (Across + SUAVE + Anoma) route every transaction to the cheapest secure venue in <800 ms
- Agents. Mixture-of-Experts running 95% on-device, 5% verified cloud bursts only when needed

- Privacy. Everything zero-knowledge by default; you can prove you paid taxes without showing income
- Interoperability. IBC + Hyperlane + LayerZero v3 mean your agent sees 400+ chains as one balance sheet

Chapter 13 - The Psychological Upgrade

"The average person today has more power in their phone to manage wealth than the richest kings in history had in their treasuries. The only thing missing is the mindset to use it."

Michael Saylor (2024)

The biggest unlock of following whats outlined in this book is not the yield, it's the peace of mind.

- You no longer wake up wondering if your advisor is on vacation when rates spike.
- You no longer dread April because the K-1s are late.
- You no longer refresh Coinbase during dinner hoping the price didn't dump while you weren't looking.
- Your entire financial life is handled by "staff" that literally never sleeps, never steals, never goes on maternity leave, and never charges you 1% to underperform the market.

That feeling is radical control without cognitive overload and its what people mean when they say "sovereign."

About the author

John Berry is a seasoned strategist, technologist, speaker, advisor and start-up founder. With over three decades of hands-on experience in technology leadership for companies including Lotus Development, IBM, Norton, and Symantec, his expertise spans cryptocurrency trading, numerous blockchain projects, cybersecurity defenses, and privacy solutions.

His journey into crypto and blockchain began in the early days of Bitcoin's adoption, likewise he was an early participant into DeFi where he also advised clients on yield farming strategies.

A vocal advocate for financial sovereignty, John bridges the gap between cutting-edge innovation and practical application. Berry's insights have been sought by industry forums and numerous early blockchain projects.

John is the author of seven books, including *Hack Proof: Protecting Your Privacy and Personal Data in the Digital Economy* and the forthcoming *The Sovereign Wallet: Blockchains, AI & Personal Financial Freedom* (January 2026), a practical guide to replacing centralized banking with secure, intelligent, self-custodial systems that compound wealth safely and privately.

He can be contacted for speaking engagements on LinkedIn or at TheSovereignWallet.com

Made in the USA
Monee, IL
04 November 2026

67378302R00085